Wake

Wake

POEMS BY *Bin Ramke*

UNIVERSITY OF IOWA PRESS Ψ *Iowa City*

University of Iowa Press, Iowa City 52242
Printed in the United States of America
http://www.uiowa.edu/~uipress
Printed on acid-free paper
Library of Congress
Cataloging-in-Publication Data
Ramke, Bin, 1947–
    Wake: poems / by Bin Ramke.
        p.   cm. — (Iowa poetry prize)
    ISBN 0-87745-658-5 (pbk.)
    I. Title.   II. Series.
    PS3568.A446W35   1999
    811'.54—dc21   98-47406

99   00   01   02   03   P   5   4   3   2   1

for Nic

Dreams—are well—but Waking's better

EMILY DICKINSON (450)

Contents

The Ruined World, 1

Essay, 11

A Theory of Fantasy, 15

Chivalric, 16

A Little Ovid Late in the Day, 19

Livery of Seisin, 20

Shostakovich and Kubatsky in Archangel, 22

Mercy, 26

Someone Whispers Below in the Garden, 29

Sad Stories, 30

Grass Fires, 31

Small Noise the Weather Makes, 33

Body Parts (1968), 36

& the War in France, 38

Another Lean, Unwashed Artificer, 39

A History of His Heart, 40

Pretty Words, Parabolas, 45

Enter Celia, with a Writing, 46

A Great Noise the World Makes, 48

A History of Tenderness, 59

For I Have Already Been Once . . . , 74

And the Light Never Waned in the Same Way Twice, 77

How Light Is Spent, 83

Toying, 85

Toy Houses in the Landscape, 87

Crisis, 90

Famous Poems of the Past Explained, 92

Testimony, 94

Notes, 113

Acknowledgments

These poems first appeared in the following periodicals: *American Letters and Commentary* (1996): "Body Parts (1968)" [*Pushcart Prize Anthology*, 1997], "Someone Whispers Below in the Garden"; *Atlanta Poetry Review* (1998): "A Little Ovid Late in the Day"; *Bloomsbury Review* (January 1995): "A Theory of Fantasy" [*Yearbook of American Poetry*, 1996]; *Colorado Review* (1996): "Chivalric," "Shostakovich and Kubatsky in Archangel," "Crisis," "Famous Poems of the Past Explained"; *Electronic Poetry Review* (1996): "Livery of Seisin"; *Germ* (1997): "Essay"; *Louisiana Literature* (1997): "Grass Fires," "Small Noise the Weather Makes"; *Missouri Review* (Spring 1995): "& the War in France," "A History of His Heart," "Pretty Words, Parabolas," "Enter Celia, with a Writing"; *New American Writing* (1998): "Daniel" (part 1 of "Testimony"); *Ohio Review* (1996): "Sad Stories," "And the Light Never Waned in the Same Way Twice," "Toy Houses in the Landscape," "Wake" (part 2 of "Testimony"); *Paris Review* (1999): Part 1 of "A Great Noise the World Makes"; *Pequod* (1995): "How Light Is Spent" [*The Best American Poetry*, 1995]; *Southern Humanities Review* (1998): "The Ruined World"; *The Spoon River Poetry Review* (1996): "For I Have Already Been Once . . ." as "Play House"; *Volt* (1996): "A History of Tenderness."

Wake

The Ruined World

(ITS GLORY)

It makes a music anyway.
It is filled with beige plants and charcoal birds
it lingers
sunsets continue, chronic circling
rain will always fall
music breaks its heart
the barren seeds feed the birds
something moves
the light of a sun insinuates
puddles gather into lakes
sounds mingle into new chords
toothed edges of dry leaves cut
it cannot be stopped
it varies inversely with the square of the distance
its lakes reflect, on calm days
it makes its noises
its despised birds fly
it continues its turnings
the light is general and various
the noise of waves in the stormy nights
the sound of anything is a cleverness

but it remains a world. A place of consequence, of sequence. I pick
up scraps of paper and smooth them, pushing with both hands flat
against my thigh. The papers are various. I carry a tool for poking
in debris. I live this way.

The ruined world is mainly gray but the occasional flash, like the epauletted blackbird you remember, is all the sweeter now for its rarity. The air has its taste and its grit. The water is always brown.

The boatmen continue to love the world. The random riches, the fish.

Across the largest lakes the tinny bells still call for the faithful, beg for forgiveness and a return to the fold. It is only the wind moving among the ruins.

Nothing has changed.

> *Like many a voice of one delight,*
> *The winds, the birds, the ocean floods,*
> *The City's voice itself, is soft like Solitude's.*

"Stanzas Written
in Dejection,
Near Naples"
—Shelley

(OVERHEARD)

Never trust the words. I do not
like the noise I make. It's all
I have, the noise I make, the trust. To make the words

a human failing. Noble silence dead. Out of the depths
I cry unto thee o lord, lord hear my voice

fade softly into the hard discussion
who wouldn't like to know
this kind of consolation

word

not threatening
to hear while
casually under sun
it sounds like

rain and shimmering
small secret life
say some

story circling its way some
where the words wind
into tight knots stop then start
over
she heard a sound

as an infant she made faint noises, was called Good Girl
later she listened to her little records
on her boxy machine, which made her happy
a girl should be happy it is a world of sunlight
and the darkness behind the door is not her fault

the sunlight is made of those particles that penetrate the ether
shadows are an absence yes but make
the same sound as light
she plays in the sunlight she plays in the sunlight
" . . . as we were walking along
introduced me without warning to his habit

of suddenly quietly singing" —John Cage
a man at a public telephone in an airport
turns to the window to appear to be observing the landscape

(Using the term "note" for a sound produced by a periodic
disturbance, there is no doubt that a well trained ear can resolve
a note into pure tones of frequencies equal to those of the
fundamental and its harmonics.
        —*Encyclopædia Britannica*)

he cries a sound or two escapes he wears a dark suit
he carries a briefcase as he turns I pretend I am reading
I watch him leave I never see him again

How did he become who he is why does he
suffer

Kant: What can I know? What ought I to do? What may I hope?

to break the heart

thee, o lord, lord hear my voice.

My talkative friend bought a bicycle in his old age;
an interesting angularity, knees and elbows,
walking stick attached to the handlebars for when he stopped.

All about bicycles he told, and about
the suicide, how hard it must have been
in that last moment down the hill to keep his aim for the tree;
the one about the policeman during the war, in
Holland, who hummed constantly, they heard him coming, and his
    enemy the artist of contraband,
how you could see a cyclist trying to escape for miles in that flat
    land;
and how the sounds of warning would carry,
and the whistling of the policeman, and the storms.

Boys say to fathers many words they have forgotten.

My father, too, knew words for things, the chemical compositions,
formulas that applied to the normal family. There was a terrible
dark form in the bottom of our bathtub, a vague shape rising
through the vitreous surface where he spilled hydrochloric acid.
He knew secrets of the soul, I am sure he did. He must have been
a man of passions, he would have told me if he could.

My friends all say there is much to talk about.
There is a sound to make that means happiness,
and there is noise to accompany tears.

When Elizabeth Bishop wrote that the beach hissed like fat, what
did she damage? Not the future, which also hisses like fat. She said
the little birds skittered along the edge of the foam, that the
particles of sand when wetted by the seawater reassemble into a
denser surface and a sound results, a continuous sigh of the beach
itself, not the ocean. Oh the ocean has been known to speak for
centuries, such a claim is commonplace. And sand is a famous
symbol, to do with time. There is nothing more to be said.

On every continent even this very night
there are children crying, telling you of their guilt.
And there are chickens climbing into their roosts
muttering to themselves, beginning to nod
even as their lovely hard feet fasten tightly,
a special tendon doing the work all night.
And all the creatures of the world sigh
into their little futures, and close their eyes
and breathe for nothing but their need, quiet.

(AMONG TREES)

Among the laurus nobilis
conspiring molecules
quiver in light

fir or feathered
a tangle of tangent
the glitters radiant

pine and parameters
quercus virginiana
festooned

tillandsia usneoides
epiphytic bromeliads
bay

growing in my mother's yard also
laurel
hemlock

the light this way
green as if
it were one

thing
green as gravity
growing

Imaginably twisting groundward
and rot and riddling a massiveness of organization
organic, roots: mirrored by limbs and twirling loose
in air movement and marauding photons glancing
as if it were possible. Nothing more, as from the bible
the love of trees something vastly and evil. Engorged.

The way to prophecy is to keep secrets.

We could speak of birds, or of air either. Ether.

A hint is powerful. The way to god is ambiguity. A path
to his house, his hovel, his shelter under the trees.

A family among the trees begins to die, the generation
having gathered, all uncles and aunts to the world, the pace
of their aging not hurried but they die and gather a smaller
group each time around the gathering graves. Soon under
a liveoak one alone will wipe his brow and turn away.

"How tender the green tip before the leaf grows."
    —Robert Duncan

The enormous deciduous climb the gradual plain
the effect the geology of it all gone
there is a glitter beneath the wires the wind
plucks them a tone emerges the shatter
beneath and like longing turned crystalline
light light light

If the clouds be full of rain, they empty *themselves* upon the earth:
and if the tree fall toward the south, or toward the north, in the
place where the tree falleth, there it shall be. *Eccles. 11:3.*

A fill of forests and the story fills
us with regret and sweetness. We love
one another. The trees are ancient
and the story is long but no one tires
listening and great libraries flutter
from each limb and there is more to read
than ever can be told and more time
from the shade of the tree saunters
in front of the following sun
and still the story lingers.

(PREFACE)

A darkening delivers us
a children's game or simply
human-shaped and sharp
a cowboy or some ethnic profile
toy soldier
formulae for anything and crowds
starlings change
shape forming and reforming against sunset

(into brightness in the dark
by the flame of his match he
felt the warmth of her hand on his
dissolve into the night the dark
he never saw such a face such
a woman smoke in the street walking)

there is your pattern of flourish
in this forest around the river
where Hansel wandered and Gretel
a flourish of blossom in the spring of fruit in the autumn
sadly slender humans descend their own nervous systems
eye to brain to spine
men do this and boys they look

(The amateur beekeeper should never work among his bees
without a veil, for stings about the face are particularly painful
and embarrassing.
            —*Beekeeping for Profit*, Randolph)

they look at
mingling with air, wave, waving there
awe and careless
through crowds of flesh the boys
look and burning with will they sell
buy and belong

(. . . it is characteristic of more refined humanity to respect "the
mask" and not to indulge in psychology and curiosity in the wrong
place.
            —"What Is Noble?" Nietzsche)

lovely and true they are
to the ways of flesh, flash and awe

and teeth and lips and eyelids and lashes
jumbled flesh earlobes the tiny maze they dangle from
and the bones beneath to shape
a thing to gaze upon

he kept his most accurate
mirror in his own room, well protected a little frightening

it is a game or toy a life. I was happy
and you were beautiful and we danced like the movies
someone did. Those were the days:

And here Aeneas saw the son of Priam,
Deiphobus, all of his body mangled,
his face torn savagely, his face and both   Aeneid 6, 651–655
his hands, his ears lopped off his ravaged temples,
his nostrils slashed by a disgraceful wound.

I would amazed listen
to the radio on the river the captains of ships conversing
the mates and enginemen the crackling
of two-way radio the rhythmic noise
and unamazed my uncle's sullen face hearing
his eyes closed his hand taking a shorthand
his understanding complete. I continued my games
hiding among the ship's stores and commerce
crates and gear to sell to passing mariners.
It seemed a game, this kind of life, of making a living
making believe, believing. This he could do
like child's play, his face behind his hand, hearing.

Essay

we might say that the secret aim of a work is to make us think it created itself by some process remote as possible from the actual.—Paul Valéry

If
all emotion is anger

words out of the
wilderness
tell my story

wither:

nothing looks like this
all dead and all
full of stars, of pinholes
and the light littered

dream: give myself
a chance

Talk Show
and Tell
the desert lies before us
pretty enough
full of air and light
I'm a boy who doesn't know much

sound and vision
and voice

dream: view occluded

it might be morning

EVERY MAN WANTS TO BE DANGEROUS

living in a boy's book anyone can be heroic making silence into
a clear preference a decision as if the very air had itself to blame
silent masses moved across the landscape—no, they made a noise
the wind announced itself
the trumpeter's music is his very breath he struck her across the
mouth she was an actress he was famous for his breath and clothes
she probably cried he was famous for his anger he was sorry in the
morning

SULLEN LIBERTIES

you can hear anything if the crowd is large enough
was his principle remember Verlaine's
Avec des *indeed* et des *all rights* et des *hâo*s
—*Sonnet boiteux*
all around the breath of men and women
boys and girls swirls full of vibration

The language of the age is never the language of poetry.—Gray

Spell it? He can't spell it. No father, no mother, no friends.—*Bleak
House*

FOSSIL POETRY
                    —Emerson

HISTORY

has tongues / Has angels has guns—Stephen Spender

> *Fran*: Nay, answer me. Stand and unfold yourself.
> *Ber*: Long live the King!

HERE

             near the mountains the
                      sun swerves hopeless
into evening   sincere
       birds waver   a person
             could use a minor friend

MINDING MANNERS

This will have to be my own story this will have to be a story this
might as well be a story
a telling   otherwise live among these ghosts wisely or well enough
        just think she said
how happy you would have been had you been
a happy person

FIRST PRINCIPLES

"The saint's love of God showed itself in his love of the poor, and
for the relief of these the young prince gave all he possessed, using
on their behalf the influence he had with his father and with his
brother Ladislaus when he became king of Bohemia. In honour of
the Blessed Virgin Mary Casimir frequently recited the long Latin
hymn '*Omni die dic Mariae*,' a copy of which was by his desire
buried with him. Though this hymn, part of which is familiar to

us through Bittleston's version, 'Daily, Daily Sing to Mary,' is not uncommonly called the hymn of St Casimir, it was certainly not composed by him, but by Bernard of Cluny in the twelfth century."—Alban Butler

"When the small boats began gathering in the evening
to take us back after work, we would begin to stand
and get our backs accustomed to it, for we had mainly
stooped for the full ten hours, except
the little time they gave for lunch. Some would
stumble into the boats like drunkards, some
would step so carefully as if into
church, noses pointed forward. Some would be
sick on the trip back home, leaning
over the gunwales and drawing up the fish which
would gather on the greasy surface as the sun set
and the stars began to burn through the little light.
No one noticed this but me, all being too tired.
I don't know why I watched this way.
I needed to know something and found the world
a good enough subject."

Everyone says his prayers
but

—*for Susan Howe*

A Theory of Fantasy

The boy his hand the size of the bird
Brilliant into the window pane the bird
The same heartbeat beat at the boy's
Wrist the folded wings. The bird revived
To stare at the view the aspens the
Mountains beyond. The bird flew and
I said You saved him. This art
Of lying we found alluring.
Boy and father staring at the aspens the
Mountains beyond.

We looked up the name of the bird studied the colors
And ranges. He tried to read the Latin like
A summer language. He failed.
As if evil were useful
He continued to dwell in that body not
Diseased merely doomed. And play to the world. Snow
Lay under the limbs of trees. The leopard lay with the lamb.
Contingencies threatened. He read himself
To sleep he dreamed spotted animals slink
Brain sex and muscle under pelt. Snow
Gathered by night by morning the world wore
Its white brain through which some crocus
Might break small and bright a language.

Chivalric

Heraldry and all its lovely language;
I chose my time there learning
elsewhere, where else than land,
Landscape, and how to live, in it
is not like, nothing is like, the colors
or the snow, it is not like pearl and
it is not like the glitter of rainwater
that darkens the bark against which
the occasional bloom-laden branch
might be seen shedding petals. No.
Here is the past: One was once a boy
and read books and could not pronounce
the most engaging words and read
in silence under blankets. Here
one was not like oneself or was
quiet and wrong and did not know
the words nor how to ask, who
to ask. Nor why. Boy's books with flags.
Everyone's born to the language; anyone
can say something. For instance,
knight banneret, that's what she called him,
having no use for him after history,
she thrust him into the operatic night:

                    A woman's hand rose
above the surface of the lake and caught
the glistering sword, and slowly

descended into the boy's refuge,
his astonishment, so foreign, so little like home.
Knights Baronets—inferior barons formed
by James I in 1611, the titles were sold
and the funds went toward the plantation of Ulster.
For this one would receive the right
to a Field argent, a sinister hand
couped the wrist gules.

How foreign she was
when God still cared. This is like a life,
like a history built fluently, as if
on the innocent, Boy-books and children's
crusades: The Reading (*al-Korân*)
versus The Writing (*Scripture*).
Isn't it interesting, east / west, us / them?
Everyone's born to something.

You should have feared
the flick of my uncle's thick wrist and
the boat rides when he took me in those days,
salt water in the bay and hard slaps against the hull;
back from a day of horizons, of shrimp nets,
I would lie on the bow feeling anger against
my whole boy's body as the engines uttered
their single syllable for twenty miles back to land,
a whine more terrible than laughter.

The oral tradition, a voice hard and horrifying.
One might have been a chevalier.

Like someone from the books, was she
beautiful? Was your mother lovely
and a kind of landscape herself, like snow
in dark woods, not like anything else?

Le plus que lent, my mother would say.
She'd say, like Debussy
she would say these things. Me
and Mom in the kitchen: I should learn
to waltz, it is a pretty thing to do
at home, a thing the body does.
The feet and blood. But mother
doesn't dance. I make up memories
but who oh love, you used to
dance; who'd kiss their hands?

A Little Ovid Late in the Day

It is late in the day
to outlive the words:
tales of incest, corruption,
any big, mythic vice
against the color of sun,
the sweetness of the time of day—
I know the story,
it is the light I care about.
The book falls from my hands
and I know all the stories,
I know better than that.
They glitter in the grass.
This is fun in the summer,
the sun descending onto my back,
the weight of eight light-minutes
warm there against skin.
Someone will read aloud to me
when I have forgotten the words,
the look they make against the page,
the kind of stain it is against the paper.

Livery of Seisin

the delivery of property into the corporal possession of a person; in the case of a house, by giving him the ring, latch, or key of the door; in the case of land, by delivering him a twig, a piece of turf, or the like.—OED

Of touch, the annoyance
That if I touch you you
Touch me—the affront it is and

Its reciprocal nature and it is
The basis of the lighter
Perversions, *frottage*, for instance, which is

The secret joy of public
Touching it is, on a bus
To transport to touch the whole self

There is no stopping
It, if (there is no defense)
I touch you you touch me

If I touch (if not you)
The glamour of the stars
Oh the stars (famously beyond reach)

That such light touches
The eyes the retina, parts of the skin
The inevitable body (where we live no matter)

And too
The warm the sun striking out
But the stars softly at night (impossibly by day)

That we touch the stars
And that any light-
Emitting body (heat, and any radiation)

Is infinite in size or will be,
Caressing the universe
At a hundred eighty-six thousand

Miles per second
O love o sacred. To change,
To hold the house in your hand, the subject,

To expand infinitely to the end
Too terrible to think upon
Each man's life is but a breath (Psalm 39) A touch

A touching most intimate,
The breath a column still attached
To the warm wet lung, every leering man knows

What he's doing, dreary,
Perpendicular sounds flying past
Touch, extensive touch of someone's tongue,

Expensive,
O do talk less, give us
Room, give us air dry and drifting

Flowers inventing
Themselves on the tips
Of trees, reach out Nature reaches

Trees reach out like
Stars light their touch
And candor, all their own. Their touch.

Shostakovich and Kubatsky in Archangel

Hymns and Psalms should be sung, lest the people should wax faint through the tediousness of sorrow.—Saint Augustine, The Confessions

Punctuated Equilibrium:

In *Truth* Stalin called his opera *chaos*;
he was displeased. It must have been cold
at the station. It was 1936. January.

*

Accidental elegance,

words

like dancing in hospital gowns
open on nakedness
health or disease.

*

Women in that country
wore black and walked bundled to church
white shells powdering underfoot.

The herons along the slow river danced for
the slaughter of pink shrimp where I found
teeth of alligators and

shards of whose pottery?

The burned-out traffic light where time
is money a dangerous dance of careful
cars taking turns. As
if we had all agreed, for instance,
to give it a name

or to walk together hand in hand in the dark
        eyes closed while anonymous fondling
                happens all around,
                    say, in
                the shrubbery.

        Any park will do, any part
                touching
that shiver of possibility
        as if music matters.

                        *

You want words to "do" something
        like hold water or prevent injury
        (cure the culture of its violence,
        the healing task of the literati),
        something like work. Instead they flit
        insectual moment to moment

        the beast I own, the body
        I was born with, heavy and hilarious.

*My own father took me to work in the swamps where he primed
pumps and after three hours took samples of the water so for most
of such afternoons he and I rowed among the alligators white herons
waded the brackish edges eating the shrimp the America of it. Parts
per million of dangerous matter.*

                        *

Failing to object conscientiously
my father volunteered for bomb disposal.
He never hurt anyone
in *his* war. "Look at the time"

he said to me when I noted
his pacific edge, this
in nineteen seventy-something,
my war raging without me.

The sun is close enough to touch.
Any source of light is
infinite in theory, in time,
stopping at nothing.

He made from a brass case—
unexploded ordnance—a lamp wired
to shine on mother's reading,
my own drawing. I copied
cartoons, Popeye a favorite
whose vegetarian anger puzzled.

                                        Light

going anyway, the evening the time

I said to him:

at school a boy unhappy in his sister's shoes
hid waiting for lunch to end class to begin
again poverty the strict master taught
many an alphabet.

Or last month he spent
school leisure kicking a tree to turn
the point of his shoe the toe of the left
shoe on his right foot (two left shoes
on sale ten cents his mother had ten cents)
pride sends a shiver down every chordate:
we sit at desks and hide
our shameful feet each behind the other.

Or the seven children have six pairs of shoes
it is a school day and raining who stays home?
They play a game intent around the table
this morning drawing lots, Oh God make us
children of quietness, and heirs of peace
said Clement, Bishop of Rome. Let Cherub
rejoice with Cherub, who is a bird
and a blessed Angel said Christopher
Smart, more crazy than that.

                          *

Worse than a love poem, logic says:
plant honeysuckle near any window she
might open on hot afternoons. At
the scene of her crime there are too
many letters

                    in her alphabet she
refuses to answer her mail all those
cards you never mailed there is re-
petition like music (the borrowed glory)

is silence (exploited rage).
Logic reigns: she called it
Catastrophe Theory

                    a mapping of continuous
elements encounter a moment when
the graph alters discontinuously
          the teased dog's smooth enragement
          until his bark turns into his bite.

Love me again.

—for Ann Lauterbach   25

Mercy

Hardness of hearts, all full of figures
of clarity glass-hard all   *How hot the sun rushes*
full of words minds   *Like fire in the bushes*
of men and women trying against
the fullness of their hard lives

hardness of hearts and John Clare
crazy. With the world. Of it.

We know why some men of Japan think
so hard of school girls the plaid jumpers
the little desks the shiny shoes the damp   *The wild flowers look sick*
determination . . . it is hard to be good   *at the foot of the tree*

Clare was good the stars are
small enough to ignore they touch us not
so easily yes they touch us light is star   *Birds nest are left lonely*
is part of the star come to be seen by me   *The pewit sings only*
my hardest companion
ship of hearts and pains

of sun and shine shinest
hard glitter you know better then
than to forgive far harder to   *And all seems*
live full fascinating yourself   *disheartened,*

the little girls have the hardest
life to fall into   *and lonely like me*
dangerous it is to be and beautiful

I would use such tools children
    rejoice   it   is a day
workmanship could not be   than the work
more valuable
more than angels

    recite to an audience

of ruminants literalists
filling themselves with whatever lies
at hand as if as if

some seasons lie
and no one knows better how to confront
the rain with its promise
contemplation,
such ennui—

there was a practice common in Europe
of eye-portraits, small compact gestures
like a little dance kept on a string
or some would have the artist paint
other parts, intimate
alliance
for war, for instance, a memorial

I would could I have such memory.

There was a practice common in Europe
called drizzling destroying
embroidery
for its gold thread to keep   winter afternoons
in a pouch as if to make more

but the practice grew out of desire
to dazzle with such excess of old gold thread
an imitation of the common women   (under dim light
who must reuse & husband resources   bending eyes badly)
the drizzlers display their gold thread & ript
apart the embroidery of the previous century
such drawing-room dazzle while gossiping   among
themselves the sounds   like rain on the roof

of ripping with little gold knives & scissors meticulous.

Someone Whispers Below in the Garden

Jemand flüstert drunten im Garten; jemand hat diesen schwarzen Himmel verlassen. —"Unterwegs," Georg Trakl

. . . someone has left this black heaven, someone
has forgotten . . . look how otherwise everyone is, how
easy it is to be happy.

This is an age when each room could be filled
with poems and music, every taxi arrive on time

I can buy three pears any morning, red ones
and green and gray and some with blue specks
like birds' eggs and some a sort of yellow
that used to be the color of Vienna

and nothing makes anyone happier than cats

and with my pears a bag of sunflower seed
to scatter and draw the birds within reach

and every window can be opened and every
sun can shine on someone or something
and the roads are clean and the trees bend

but blue in the evening the rage rings
among the little trees in the toy forest,
the feral creatures tremble and wait for me
to offer my guidance, to spread
my arms and welcome them back
oh happy afternoon oh tiny grandeur.

Sad Stories

He was born in a basket, he carried his own bones
in a bag. A man prone to purity, he was a ghost.
Such a sad story, why do you listen?

You see that saying is believing, piety the easiest
delusion. Isn't it a kind of failure, all these words
like the Bible says? Oh that my head were waters

and mine eyes a fountain of tears, Jeremiah wrote,
that I might weep night and day. And they bend
their tongues like their bow for lies. I like that one.

So it is a small story that has a moral and a hero
who loves children and there is clarity and precision
throughout the land. No more hunger. Or

only hunger, there is nothing but hunger, appetite
survives and that is the moral of the story. Writing
about the need of the people, and turning

the story into anything, dance & music for instance,
and then we are happy as anything living the life
of leisure, the pen in her hand, her very hand a ballet.

Tell me your terrors, she said to me that first night,
that woman of will and wisdom, for a hundred dollars
per hour, more or less. We spoke of terror

and tenderly shivered together as if no one before
had ever known. It's allowed, she said, there's
a war on. And we wept together like Jeremiah.

Grass Fires

It is hard that way, crushing
and consuming the world, a tangible fabric's
febrile embrace—nothing safe. It's dog eat
or be eaten. The landscape swerves—I awake
this morning as if I know something and I love
the way it makes me feel dangerous. The loud
world listens. I as farmer. No one
knows better how it moves, the earth, into itself,
sensible to the harrow, the plow, the pitiless hoe.

Such burning. It is morning.
Burn something down, or up.
I am so afraid of myself
it is hard to get up in
the morning the bright
burning burning.
Or it is simply summer, it is hot but
not burning, I do not
believe.

All the old heroes were failures at home.
Laughably lachrymose fellows, they rowed
across the salty Middle-of-the-Earth
to get somewhere else fast, faster than that.
A way to spend the winter, with someone
else's fire and wife. Burning fields of grain, grasses,
burning the storage sheds, burning the barns.
Dogs will eat dogs and babies will cry
jaws open and the wind whistling, silly wind.

Yet I have seen women burst
brave into flame in the streets.
And one night I with a beautiful one
as we touched all the dangerous
places we heard on the radio another one
burst into flame in the streets
and we laughed knowing
nothing else to do than burn
burning up the night threatening

every horizon with light and my own
childhood heroes still trail
behind me, bride that I am,
a train, something like a veil,
burning burn her own hair, my
face on fire, the world in mourning
before it knew all was ablaze.
He feedeth on ashes. Isaiah 44:20

On the end of tender green stalk
a flame a flower. I love nothing but gardens.
I fear nothing but myself I am no gardener. I
can be quoted aflame afire a friend to fear
fallen away, alone burning.

Small Noise the Weather Makes

Nostalgic for metaphor she pared her shimmered
life into lacquered packets. Her story
circled its way somewhere, dim where
words wind into tight knots, stop, then start.

Focus on a sound, the fountain behind the voice,
of any water: the drift of rivers and rain.
Even to hear the splash of coffee is a choice
against her, against such past tense.

A moment ago she saw the ring of bone
around her own eyes then she darkly
moved into her skull's damp domed
gravity, searching for the trace of fissure

trace of metaphor and a reason to live,
a fine delicacy, a step in a straight line.
What the maid saw, it would give
a man the creeps, would straighten your hair

would make your sister weep. She has things
to do, but if she spoke cars would crash
on wet pavement, wheels would bring
glorious fatality against a threat of sun.

No threat, the weather not threatening, just
the mumble she heard while glamour casual
under sun waited for the bus she must
wait for her friend, a future to take home.

Hers is history, how it sounds; waiting for bed
what did she love? Remind her.
And so it occurs to me to say, she said,
There is danger of death by traffic,

danger in events, of arrest for violations,
for all the sounds of music. She must
trust a sensible chaos. Weather. You can listen:
Father would in the morning

pin on himself a picture of himself
after dressing for work. Prepared
to make his way, his day divided
neatly itself as I went to school

he went orderly badged to work forever.
A place in line on her island no longer
volcanic, eruptions are not weather.
The world resists wetly. *Here is what sex was like:*

the sunlight shimmers, the sun as if wet
shimmers across a lightly wetted back
the brown skin and the blood beneath and breath
held, held, then gone, dead the last home

from work they have their badges on,
their little pictures, fathers,
of themselves, not smiling much. And when
the weather cleared they would begin

again: *tour boats would speed down our river.*
We rushed to watch their passing, dark water
rise against the riverbank, the land itself
dissolved into the river, the land rose

precipitate on the other side, our poor place
ever smaller dissolving where we lived but
we loved the boats anyway, the movement,
the speed and slender arrogance of sharp

pointed boats passing us a person aboard
waving to us, and I loved him more than even
the smell of diesel in my small wet cortex,
the little ship would pass from sight turning

as on a heel, a toe, turning its wake to us against
us children there waving, on shore
for want of nothing, for love of the way
the water moves, the sound it makes.

—for Rick Ramke

35

Body Parts (1968)

HISTORY

Divided and divided and again against
itself, the body the body. Meiosis and other
forces in the tiny universe, so
solemn and satisfied. Here is a war for you.
In school they would wear fatigues
and say *I was there*. And they were, and are. We trembled
in their wake, wondering. We studied *here*. No *there*
was worth the work and still we suffered.
Where was I? To see is just to see.

THEOLOGY

And then there was God, and the newest theory
and the finest film of desire began to appear
in their eyes, mistaken for tears. A prayer
that would suffice.
There was a time the women
dressed in desire and the men
in meaning, when no one listened
to anything
willowy lingering
wails announced the foreign about to fall
at their feet. Some nice
new accents might arrive
with marble and Italians to carve it, white

blasted from big holes
in the native soil. Full of history is
hard country. There's work across the sea.

ART

Smooth as stone and turn upon turn
surrounds the glister of flesh
monumentally other the only
the library's Psyche the memory
of marble though carved
anything can last
forever, given time enough. Obstacles
strung between us from the start
like wasps flung across the path at a pretty
party, like flagstone. The views, you would say,
some limb severed you still care about
because gone and long missed so nothing else
matters. They were married that way, or we
were at someone's wedding, marbled
and cool in the afternoon under tribal tents
rented metal cool to the touch to sit on.
Champagne, a color, something like that.

& the War in France

"My father dancing, my father dead," he said.
Or he did not; it is fall and flimsy leaves descend
so persistent to cause unwary reminiscing—
remember the days of dancing, or of not dancing;
rather remember the regret we planned:
going to my own grave I will say, "If only
I had danced, even once, with her, me
who never learned to live so foreign."

So hard it was, the war and all those words,
those hard words all forgotten, all that forgiving
to do. Unless, unless, as the merchant said,
"No, my good lord; he speaks the common tongue
which all men speak with him."
But I never danced with her, and she danced
when she was young, she danced I know
she told me so, she danced. We do not speak.

Another Lean, Unwashed Artificer

I could not believe in god whose ghost
would not believe in me. I became
translucent. The current century was
the shortest on record but is becoming
just like all the others, like any child
changing, grateful, predictable.
When we use words like *love* or *Saturday*
we hope for something: from the periphery
enters your vision a vision of cheap delight,
the drama of all words being the wisdom
withheld, as in *I love you.*
But everybody means everything once.
A pattern for pathos: bastard boys and
arrogant aunts and all of Shakespeare
crawling about.

A History of His Heart

Watch work being done by
a huddle of sacristans spooning   *R.C. mass with props*
incense into small machines burning.   *and God watching*
Then mixing water and wine,
miraculous cousins of blood
and semen. Work being done
and you as witness, the heart as
worker incessant within the wicked   *a Western koan*
and the good, the goofy heart pumping   *a tree falls, etc.*
like tree trunks thumping onto the forest's   *no witness*
soft floor where nobody watches work being done.

The heart is no heart in shape
nor passion: there in the dark a tree   *see Rilke (a tree*
roots to each cell capillaried limbs   *—O hoher Baum im*
responsive to weather, to seasonal   Ohr—*in the ear)*
work being done: a change

of heart inclines us. Climb
into the branched vessel bleeding;   *the metaphor*
the uses of art   *extended*
anger and allegory fill the books,   *expounded*
the modern cardiology; what work

gets done in there: listen
to wind in the lungs, the heavy   *the thoracic*
humid weather in your chest   *organs a community,*
where good neighbors huddle.   *a world.*

The examined life is unlivable.
New proofs for old theorems
on the dilemmas of history: what
is worth the effort? Love and dinner.

see Aristotle
see New Testament

"What a refined expression of love . . .
would we see in the act of a prince
who . . . sent a portion of his meal to
a pauper? And what if he sent him
his entire meal? And what if he
sent him his own arm to eat?"

*St. Francis de Sales
quoted by Alfonse de
Liguori quoted by
Piero Camporesi,
translated by Anna
Cancogne*

He felt rather than tasted the trickled
blood, its warmth; he tested the loose
tooth with his tongue and thought of
his mother. His first loss the single
bronzed shoe, then the lock of hair
she put in the book, then the dried
umbilicus curled onto the page as if
it had crawled there to die. He knew
she would want the tooth so he savored
the blood his own taste and truth. This
is not thinking, this is the unexamined
life.

*"The precisions of fate,
nothing fobbed off, nor
changed, in a beau
language without a
drop of blood."*
—Wallace Stevens

*

The glamour of dangerous words, she said—
was it a warning? The consuming self, the material
girls, or someone reading late in the afternoon.
He had an uncle who left home to find work
at age fourteen and found it. And for his full
life worked. And the boy sat on the uncle's knee

wanting him to read faster, more words more
and the uncle trying as hard as his hard hands
could to read: there was an old woman lived
under a hill, and if she's not moved
she lives there still.

*

Inside is empty as always walls keeping
    it so
out outside still cold against glass.
          Still, boys play out there
throw balls, some carry out chairs
    onto the lawn. Still clouds come
        as if whistled for.
I can't stand to listen please
    don't make more words, look
        there go words
or kites cold on wind. Inside is empty.
    The boys go home having
        lost the ball they drag
in chairs leaving the lawn to itself.
      Inside, a young man watches opera.
      In his comfortable chair.
He wonders about the lake of tears
    behind one door
        tears of dread
or of remorse? The weeping of wives
    or of Bluebeard? All castles
      are dark against the light.
Nothing is that easy. A wall
    can disappear against the light.

*

I.e., inside is a boat, outside is   *there is always*
appearance.   *a word for*
'Zebrage' the French call it. Painted   camoufleurs
warship designs from the Dada. Angular
bright surreal ships steaming above
submarines, dazzle
disappearing in the distance under light.
(As a patriotic favor Disney painted
his neighbor's roof, Lockheed hangars as
an American suburb (would Japanese
pilots crossing a Pacific know barbecue
grills, patios, pools, a California
if they saw one?)) Inside is a small
reason to live.

*

"My consuming lust to experience their
bodies," he said. So we watched the cannibal
hear his words read back while generalized
humanity watched him listening to someone
tell on him. I was young once and knew   *from the*
what it meant to want a body to lie with/on   *confessions*
to listen to its heart/beat. Consuming   *of Jeffrey*
passions and a life in rhetoric.   *Dahmer*

Inside is a small reason to live. His
ambition to be anonymous made him pale
and served him well. He still looks like
anyone painting himself into every corner.

Here is a version of history: they talk
about you then they talk to you then
you talk back.

*

I saw this: beauties of displacement   *the angels*
a man peeled his orange while water flowed   *are sorry for*
into his sweeping machine; he dropped   *their failure to*
orange peels into the gutter in front   *exist: they beg*
of the sweeper while water flowed   *forgiveness*
from the hydrant as the man peeled and
ate an orange filling his sweeper
dropping the golden acid in glowing
strips just where his gathering will
begin and behind him a clean
width will gleaming go.

—*for Donald Revell*

Pretty Words, Parabolas

A sudden telephone peeled sleep from
the household—a death somewhere and a father
left home, the long drive through morning
Tennessee gray—Or did I read it? Was it not
no, never my family's death? The old

do die, and the young. Here's a happy thought.
Happiness coheres, look at the past, as if:
once upon a time. To have a small lawn in a
large world is a victory. One kind. A place
for poppies, gentians, and a sound of water
pleasing and mountains, clouds et cetera.

If you sit to admire, to what will you turn
your back? A house, an interior and glass,
this will do. At last the world is glister
of its own making, sufficient machine. Not
at last. There is (no?) that same hummingbird
I met last summer. Learn to live.

If the Body is a form
of itself over time, then there is music, or
could be. From this pleasant prospect
we can see more air than anything. Moving.
Still my ignorance is no bliss at all.

Enter Celia, with a Writing

You have said; but whether wisely or no, let the forest judge
We continue to attend to truth as we see it.
We are a small group of humans, full of good
intentions. We are full of despair.
We continue to read ourselves to sleep at night.
We live through the nights full of desolate desire.
We have kitchens and small animals for company.
We are as good as any, better than some.
We have thought about our lives, and now it is dawn.

*

Dans mon pays, on ne questionne pas un homme ému.
(In my country, we are discreet around men in tears;
in my homeland, we observe the decorum of private grief;
back where I was born, men did not show their feelings;
surely you will not disturb me in my hour of anguish.)

The French, or such a Frenchman as that, fill their dawns
with angry art and intricate analysis. It is a way to be,
and certainly you yourself could learn something:
for instance, what of the dead Father you never buried,
and the Mother you will not allow to die? Won't
you accept his good advice, his friendship?

And what do you know about Mr. Char
and his little poems whose delicate directions
might also say with him *Les branches sont libres*

de n'avoir pas de fruits (and if the branches of my trees
are thusly liberated, why not call it triumph, why
not eat? No nation is more hungry than the French.)

*

It is not my fault. Blame yourself, this art
is not what it used to be. We grow old in debt
and no child smiles when we fall apart

no child ever sees it happen. They dangle
their charms in front of each other, they burn
with a hard, gemlike flame. The acute angle
of their anger dissipates the affection of poor
parents — they never say thank you — and the parks
are full of their demons arranging flowers fewer

care about each year. When was a rose
last named for a poet? Who cares for art
unless on stage, whose child knows

how to do anything small and discreet?
Not that it matters: all small wars wither
into family, and the State weeps in the streets.

A Great Noise the World Makes

A

Ardea Candidissima, Snowy
Heron or White
Egret, printed in London, 1835, not
the Great White, evil-
eyed with savaged prey in beak but
the one with the hunter
tiny figure, slipping forward
from the background. Figure/ground
: to the privileged eye

the bird appears to see us, ("See
how it follows you
around the room")
(I'll make a quick story:
the bluecoated figure
topping the rise halfway
between the verandahed tiny
house and the yellow-
footed bird, a distance
of seven inches, is Audubon
himself, gun in hand intending
to study, abetted by
the distracting audience.)

Of the white birds he drew
this one whitest,
something Chinese in the

composition. The sky
on this edge of America
is jungled air
along the bayous—the boil
of insects rises as the sun
sets—the night random
with nesting birds
that test the darkness from time
to time, that raise a small ruckus.

I collected feathers, kept
the herons' in a ginger jar
though they were broken, cast
off for good reason. We called all
such birds cranes and watched
with no purpose their constant crossings
the dangling Ys of legs,
their sleek S necks and
the soft incised Ws in the mud.
Is there a difference between speaking
and not speaking?
Between sound and

silence in other words?
A past determined so severely
the present that he could not wait?
Someone gazing softly
into the hard distance would know
to avoid this kind of attending,
this Nature. *Natural*
being our word for *necessary*.
Like killing time. Inserting
wires through the fresh corpse's
limberest parts—especially the neck,

the machined armature turns
beast into pliant mimesis.
Don't you just love anyone
who wants everything,
or at least one of each kind? Any
collector, say. Life-list
long as your arm. He wanted
to draw every kind of bird
in America. Noah
merely followed orders, but this
Frenchman suffered, walked
to New Orleans from Kentucky,
drew portraits of Creoles then tutored
their children for money. Meanwhile

drew birds and birds and birds.
Lovely little landscapes
beneath their craning necks,
for instance,
or sometimes small dramas,
a Laocoön of nestlings and snake.
The flat land of watercolor
teeming with rubrication and
all sorts of imitation, shimmer
and sheen. A thing to make,
a book of birds flattened, paper
covered with ink, printed and bound,
darkened with covers and collation.
It was never quiet
there, among the streaks
and daubs. Always they spoke
to him; no, but
screeched and squawked and screamed.

Few noises made by birds,
real or imagined, can be
called music. Mostly anger and fear,
sometimes lust, induces
the piteous or the terrifying timbre.
A frenzy of desire
collects reversing shadows
and reflections in a dew drop,
then dries to powder on the page.
The work men do,
and the mending required:
birds rise that way, they fly.

B

. . . and the world seemed to me a great wilderness.

—John James Audubon

Say
"I am vision" or see
limnal
as in, home, what was called happily
home
a place limnetic
boundaries bordered
by Mexican waters   the Gulf
flying fish before the boats
sent them up   mica glitter
and aerodynamic flutter fin
fear taught them
aeronautics I thrilled
to their panicked leaps
frolic and

*. . . and a pink waistcoat, from
the bosom of which, amidst a
large bunch of the splendid
flowers of the magnolia,
protruded part of a young
Alligator, which seemed more
anxious to glide through the
muddy waters of some retired
swamp than to spend its life
swinging to and fro among
folds of the finest lawn. The
gentleman held in one hand
a cage full of richly-plumed
Nonpareils.*★

★ *Passerina ciris*

51

read during leisure about lines
vertical and infinite
an inclined line infinite as necessary
sliding along another line and *rising*

> *ever higher*
> *as its angle decreased, for it*
> *was impossible for it to slip off*   the axiom of
> *and the point of their intersection,*   parallels
> *together with his soul, glided upwards*
> *along an endless path*—Vladimir Nabokov, *The Defense*

there was one Monsieur Didier we didn't
know him well—he drew pictures
of the last likely borders, the bridges
too and the lyrical
like maps it was a region   *All this raised my curiosity to*
of anxiety   *such a height that I accosted*
wet wilderness a pleasure   *him with, "Pray, sir, will you*
it could dissolve anything   *allow me to examine the birds*
piers porches any hulls   *you have in that cage?" The*
fire itself would swallow itself   *gentleman stopped, straightened*
into a thin line rising   *his body, almost closed his left*
radiant dark into   *eye, then spread his legs apart,*
let's think about the light   *and, with a look altogether*
wanting it to be Europe, anywhere   *quizzical, answered, "Birds, sir;*
not here green light and parallels   *did you say birds?" I nodded,*
the axiom of parallels no comfort   *and he continued, "What the*
soaring inarticulate   *devil do you know about birds,*
vision   *sir?"*

It is only possible to read literature all at once, totally,
not only all that has been written, but all that ever will.

Unless we engulf the entirety of this monster in one swallow,
like the tablespoon of medicine, as our mothers told us to,
it will not work and we will be condemned to piecing
absurdly together the simplest meanings of the most
obvious words, over and over again, often in the same sentence,
until the lights finally in their mercy fade
and we can turn away. Such words as "read"
and "write" and "mercy." And "and."

(He said as a boy in France he would save his drawings through the
year to burn on his birthday. A fresh start. He later learned English,
obsessively wrote, letters and journals, most of them burned by a
diligent daughter. I know other stories of burnings, other burnings
of stories the family wants quelled, quieting the translation. Carrying
across from Saint Domingue to France to America again and from
French to English—and how many names? *Fougère*, fern, during
the Reign of Terror . . . *Was not the lost dauphin, though handsome
was only / Base born. . . .* —R. P. Warren)

There is no reason to write. (The grand birds did cross the sky
a script a hand writing)

Reading tells itself that it exists, and thus, it does.

In the wet, the swamp
palmetto frond
and French curses when
the briar surprises against the wrist   *Sure enough, thought I, little*
or neck   the   *or perhaps nothing do I know*
mosquito laden air   *of the nature of those beautiful*
the taste of   *denizens of the air . . . "Sir,"*
                                           replied I, "I am a student of

listening	*Nature, and admire her works,*
and	*from the noblest figure of man*
opening	*to the crawling reptile which*
of the eye	*you have in your bosom."*
	—Journals

To reconnect; to place the pieces back into original unitary configuration; to return the amputee to prewar wholeness; to heal; to hide the seams of what was once one; to seduce into self. Remember.

Anceps: New Latin for "indeterminate": there is also a lovely term, *syllaba indifferens,* or in Greek, *adiaphoros,* for a syllable that can be either long or short at the end of a line—and some people speak of a kind of being or not-being which coalesces out of the electron-mist at the instant you think to look for it.
I was a child and my brother was a child and we argued whether there was a line beneath that mark of graphite he had made on the paper—I said no, and meant it, and thought it mattered, that you couldn't trap it ghostlike so easily as just that. He was becoming an engineer and annoyed with me. I think often these days of my faith in the abstract, my need for it; how at night it kept me warm and dry.

Listen	I was for a time apprenticed to a
I would listen	German who knew them at the
what birds—sometimes black	Bauhaus, a sculptor; I inserted
bear—in the swamp	shims in clay mixed plaster cut
stand still still	forms made boxes to transport casts
stand as the wind	to the foundry he pinned drawings
shifts sounds your (my) way	covered the walls of the studio
great birds & small	S-shapes serpentine Hogarth's
and snakes	favorite he made herons of bronze

and foliage
all as if in the mouth
melange   separating
unraveling the rope
the world is   and petals
            He had been hired

                               by the WPA to encrust
the embodiment of a theory   the post office with
of the good   the body   heroic sculpture face-
on which to inscribe incise   less torsos and blank
words no one word   stares classical as hell
only   love   sharp-edged still
                of granite in New Orleans
                it was work and grand
                and you can see it today
                he has been dead for
                        decades his work is
                        there I last saw those
                        cane cutters
                               from the bus it was late
                               at night they cast long
                               bas-relief shadows
                               he always loved
                               texture magnolia against
                               stone and the sharpest
                               angles of light the little
                               machinery of the eyes
                               busy busy
                               bronze petals
I would walk through   of magnolia
the same swamps Audubon
walked watching
for the same species of egret

55

ardea occidentalis the tiny
landscape under the wing
he loved
a world   I wanted
to know something
I was a child
beyond the swamp the Gulf
of Mexico   Mexico beyond
the flying fish leap they fall
back
Flying fish before the boats—panic
sent them up—mica glitter
and aerodynamic, fin flutter—
fear taught them
aeronautics—I thrilled
to their panicked leaps, frolic
fish can fly
"acquired Sorrow"

For six years now he had heard the
best of all talking. It was of the
wilderness . . .

—William Faulkner

(—J. J. Audubon quoted by R.P.W.)

In my city great herds of geese
        soil the walks in the parks
                infect the shallow ponds
they speak in tongues—close
        your eyes listen at
                night they arrive
more & more from Canada they
        like it here they
                like us they
will stay forever

"Master. / If you saw a bullet / hit a bird . . ."—E. Dickinson

56

*I had watched their evolutions, their gentle patting of the sea when on
the wing, with the legs hanging and the web extended, seen them take
large and long ranges in search of food, and return for bits of fat
thrown overboard for them, I had often looked at different figures
given by scientific men; but all this could not diminish for a moment
the long-wished for pleasure of possessing one in the flesh. I fired, and
dropped the first one that came alongside, and the captain most
courteously sent for it with the yawl. I made two drawings of it; it
proved to be a female with eggs, numerous, but not larger than grains
of fine powder. . . . During many succeeding weeks I discovered that
numbers flew mated side by side, and occasionally, particularly on
calm, pleasant days caressed each other as Ducks are known to do.*
                              —"The European Journals, 1826–29"

I walked alone, sometimes with a dog,
listening to my own body swerve into itself
like a nation, an adolescence brewing damage
while language hanged itself among the cypress
while long-billed curlews hid in salt grass—new moon,
the letter C glittering after snails and such small fish
as can be caught. I saw the dance of the Little Blue Heron
and I heard its wing and I saw its blue beak

I suppose I did love them like Saints
in winter when they lived among us.

C

The vaguest   the sharp-   the wrong-
ness   the shepherd of memory the sharpness
the generation of memories of birds
        recollection of birds crossing

the minds of birds teeming with visions of Canada
Coastal Texas heat & insects
the buzzing in a boy's head
fifteen birds left in all the world
imagined them above me all of them
taller than me   crossing
from the sharp C-shaped coast below us
      to Canada   we were wilderness
together   the giant birds &
the tiny boy listening

Whooping Crane

they stood five feet tall   *Grus americana*
they call across the marshes   breeds north-central Canada
they eat forever and devour   winters on Texas Gulf coast
everything like Time   alligators   *—Havell plate CCXXVI*
grasshoppers   cicadas   ghosts

white birds tall as I was, taller
white feathers brutal against
the dark the weight the light of stars and one moon
glisters against the hard geometry
shiver of sound
nothing is invincible   fifteen birds only left
call among themselves   lonely?
in the world   small world
eating and   pairing and calling
into a boy's wide   -eyed mind
dream and desire   they are gone
to Canada   home or
how the sound continues a bell a voice crying
in the wilderness.

—for my brothers and sisters

A History of Tenderness

We dream—it is good we are dreaming—
It would hurt us—were we awake—
But since it is playing—kill us,
And we are playing—shriek—
  —Emily Dickinson (531)

She'd just sit there rethinking her childhood
    waiting for the chance to get it right, knowing
        no one would make this first try
    count, *personne* is so cruel, surely.

Music might save us. Someone loved Jacqueline
    du Pré, everyone loves Elgar.
        The cello she played
    was old, and she did so young die,

lamented by Dugan,
    "cello death" he wrote of, and of
        joking away the horrors.
    Everyone loves a good death among

the neighbors. To live in a body, words and destinies:
    she never asked for any, and
        such a danger it has become
    to have one, a site for disease and desire.

Anyone could invent a past more worthy
    some spare afternoon. A windy afternoon.
        The molecules
    quiver in the sunlight the trees

the whirling arrogance of the physical determined
        to fill the moments. Nothing here is the subject:
                the difference between
        talking and not talking. Speech and silence.

Of my own ambition to be Audubon, I will not speak.
        "The bird, far from its name, flies
                from the name that I give it"
        If later there was the woman from New Orleans

and we were too young but together and so
        stayed forever when the world raged
                beyond its own edges, little wars
        washed at their beaches.

Climb trees with crayons, and
        a notebook on a looped string.
                Wedge among the limbs and watch
        the ordinary birds while the dream birds

in the books make one cry. Such sweet failure.
        " . . . but continues to fly in treatises on zoology
                and the poems of St. John Perse.
        The gull is in its sky, irreducible to ours . . ."

Who could dream it up, and who wouldn't die
        for such a world? All full of bitter beauties
                and abilities to fly.
        The bad ocean of childhood,

more mud than mystery, faces south, small
        sharks circle beneath the flat waves of the Gulf.
                A little family stands there holding hands,
        ankle deep in ocean, watching the gray sky

and the circling gulls laughing. Not
    holding hands, hands folded
        neatly each into a self, staring
    off into the world below the gulls.

". . . but the language of the taxonomist
    is in the books, itself irreducible to any
        gull ever dreamed of,
    living or dead."—Bruno Latour.

Notes: Bruno Latour is French. *Personne*
    is French. My mother is French,
        Cajun, diminished
    heir to a preliterate culture,

a dark people well disposed to shadows
    and eerie childhoods, prone
        to accidents, often wearing
    hearts on sleeves.

No one knows. Everyone speaks.
    One day I learned the earth's surface
        does move
    and Brazil did fit into Africa

the sun was shining and small mammals
    ingeniously opened various
        types of nuts.
    The children were feeding

bread to geese. On such a day one might learn
    anything, but some days
        I am simply delighted to
    finish a sentence, and all

the words fit, and no offense taken.
Like a Spaniard she wrote poems
to save a nation, a minimal casualty:
thinking in Italian, she despaired.

Thinking she was Egyptian
she died, desiccated, dreamed:
"To live is to live forever;
to die is to never have been."

She would like to return
to the egg to inscribe her mourning
sickness, her glorious
health of habit her secret street

self, graffito of further desperations.
Morning the flower —
a weed, really — over
her shoulder we see against

if you focus beyond, the morning glory
blue of ocean, gray, it
must be summer already,
good heavens. "And I remember

sharp Japonica — the driving rain."
Spring was invented there
across that ocean
ten years ago. No one knew better

so the idea spread. You'd think some day
someone would stop it,
would return to the old
ways, the snow and wolves.

If you turn this weather into wisdom
　　　you will hold the answers
　　　　　dear and distant beyond
　　　that line of cypress, tooth-edged

against the sky. If He has sent you to bind
　　　up the brokenhearted, to proclaim
　　　　　liberty to the captives,
　　　He's made a mistake.

The weather is readied for spring
　　　and we children wander untidy
　　　　　picking at our small
　　　poverty worn like Style, outlaws of mercy.

Listen to sad stories: Once upon a time
　　　the man who could not speak
　　　　　to his wife feared her rejection
　　　so everyone sleeps alone in his house.

All these parables of capitalism, all
　　　words and words. The laughter
　　　　　cartoonish can rise like bubbles
　　　fish breath forming domes in water.

Perpendicular sounds fly above us.
　　　Still, the old virtues come home to roost.
　　　　　If a herd of sinuous tumbleweed
　　　weave onto the interstate at seventy

miles per hour still words come to mind:
　　　dendrite, scarf-joint, fishplate. Fiche,
　　　　　"to fasten." Morning glory
　　　penetrates the topiary

like words the bristling brain. No words.
    "I remember it well in my
        mother's apartment.
    It was in the living room

on a wall facing Fifth Avenue over
    an unused fireplace" John Whitney
        Payson, on Van Gogh's
    Irises, recently auctioned.

Purple and green maybe bruised words auctioneer's
    the air around them thick
        as paint the way things
    continue temporarily.

The name on the bottom of the blind
    is "Del Mar." He sees it
        when he opens the window
    at night to spill cool air

onto his bed. He doesn't sleep and doesn't
    read. He sees the ceiling. The casual
        fit of the quarter-round
    to the tiles and walls; the corner

especially annoys after two A.M. when
    he will turn off the lamp,
        the tiny light
    clipped to the headboard, too soon,

then will lie in the dark imagining.
    He does still see darkly
        her face of twenty-
    five years ago; the slender woman

wore eyeliner and walked unafraid
   the dark streets of New Orleans
      at two A.M. He will two
   or three times a day invite

that picture of her waiting for him
   she a person in a street
      alone like a forest
   nobody there, *personne*,

that image of her waiting, she
   sitting on the ledge of a shop window
      like any streetwalker
   her hair short angular like black and white

movies. Like France. The blind was
   blue on the room side, white
      for the neighbors. It was
   paper like something Japanese and folded.

There has been no sex since the birth
   of the only child. No anger, no
      discussion. Nothing left
   to say, not "slept together."

(He tells himself this is not his worst
   behavior: it could be true. He waits
      naked on the table
   cold as medicine for her arrival

whose routine never varies except for the sex.
   She tries to remember
      the last time. He loves it
   all, even the standing in the grim

steel corridor knowing they all are watching.
    The oldest Korean woman
        opens the inner door
    with the greeting, "Forty dollar."

One of the girls rises from the mat on which
    they lie to watch TV, smiles and
        takes his arm. It used to be
    a different girl each time, but now

it is always Kay. Or Qué. Or K. Her touch.
    She asks about his health, his
        family. She no longer reminds
    him of her tip. When he hands her the pack

of twenties, she is efficient as any receptionist,
    points to the little pegs for hanging
        his shirt and pants above,
    his sad little shoes side by side below.

There is no window, but the partition walls
    do not reach the ceiling. He is
        on his stomach.
    He does not look at the ceiling.)

In earliest months of marriage he began his affair
    with Ariadne, who was never
        present when it happened,
    who smiled at the weakness of men,

the folly of appetite. He and Ariadne
    and her father had dinner
        at a restaurant thought
    to have once been a brothel.

Her father never paid income tax
        thinking so long as one never appears
            a name on the records
        one remains safe. His daughter's

date, this married man, after the veal, became
        nervous under the portraits hanging
            in the Smoking Room,
        the red-lined room with brandy.

He refused the offered cigar, and the older
        men smiled, everyone seated,
                quiet, confident.
        He spent the end of the evening

with Ariadne in a borrowed room of the Pontalba.
        He was pleased to be in the building
            that he'd admired
        distantly on postcards. The apartment

disappointed, but not its balcony from which
        one could hear St. Louis Basilica
            chime, and pigeons
        whir airborne, and the various

dangerous sounds of ships on the Mississippi
        lying higher than the land itself
            between levees. He
        leaned with both hands on the iron rail

listening to all warnings, thinking how
        beautiful his wife was,
                dark and filled
        with some past of her own

even if the good stories were taken,
all told, and all the good
people dead. There's
nothing to do but the talking long

into someone's night like an old joke.
Innocence is a dangerous
hobby, not for
the amateur, the happy husband who loves

like music. Everyone loves Jacqueline
du Pré, everyone loves Elgar.
The cello she played
was old, and she dead so young,

among the neighbors, there is music, too,
adagia played moderato, for
instance, no joke,
Elgar's cello concerto, like,

like something, like nothing, no word
for it . . . it is about no word,
nothing. No one, or
personne, can hear her sawing away, still

in that damned machine, at that box
of air (she was six years younger
at her death than I
am now, imagine it) that furniture

more costly than anything I've slept in
eaten on, written on,
or loved beneath.
I love all women of fifty years.

It was such a pretty box of air she played
    there was almost weather in it.
        "I felt as if I
    could not breathe"—Pablo Casals.

I, too, wish it were music. You can hardly
    go wrong there, in their
        world: everyone
    loves you if you practice, years of practice

it takes and why not, the years will pass anyway.
    Think of the terrible machinery
        it takes to make
    a poem. The books collecting for forty years

the shelves, the humming computer on the pretty
    desk, the power to organize, oh,
        the human genome, to
    organize weather. The ink. The lamp. The cat.

The awful rug and the spindly spider plant kept,
    mites and mitochondria, through
        the winter. But today
    is a nice day and the sun shines.

That the world is mathematical. No. That the world
    is describable mathematically. But
        describable is an ugly word.
    But no word is ugly. What is *ugly*, the word?

What beyond the politics of it, the philosophy? Last
    night I ate half a banana, picking
        small pieces off the shaft,
    inching the thick skin down yet still

unable to induce appetite. This morning the tropical
    smell of it thickens the air around
        the table. The shape
    of anything, of nothing, that graph

the self is of its progress through—Time? Air?
    Molecular disarray? Dawn, which is
        continuous, a slow
    disrobing of phallic presence, lunging

(lounging) in the dark (into the dark) dawn means
    nothing, the world a map of
        itself mapping
    one-to-one ratios a clear symptom.

You know how lavender such air feels on
    such mornings after, the iris in bloom and
        it all makes a person
    want to climb something, mountains

sometimes, ice covered. Sometimes they fall. Still, it's
    no safer to have ideas: the man
        in the park on his bench
    has ideas and could be happy under the sun.

In the park the old ambition makes it pretty:
    clay pots, masses of annuals, wallflower,
        forget-me-not,
    polyanthus, primula, convulvula, lots

of nasturtiums and a red brick path with moss
    under an actual magnolia.
        A boy and girl
    in a city by the river getting married

and the light reflects off the basilica, entire
     ecstasies rise. Glory. It mattered
         who was young,
       who still alive, and what lingered.

For that betrayal in the Pontalba he desired her
     forgiveness. When the decades passing
         made it safe
       to ask, she could not remember the offense,

so could not forgive. Or I wish it were the movies,
     the left hand of the editor white and
         lintless, gloved like
       no one's dream. Hope is anyone's in

the movies, the editor cuts and pastes all day, long
     strips of art and history to run in his
         machine backward and
       forward like time at the atomic level of Indian uprisings

and submarine sinkings bombs float upward
     into the bellies of airplanes like eggs
         returning and polished
       pots spin back into clay his hand is clean

and his art is absence. "It is absence that
     receives us"—Edwin Muir. Editing as history.
         A museum returns
       its Indian art: figures and weapons, pots and sand.

Retrieved by tribes for returning to plein-air shrines all
     to dissolve in the great gift cycle.
         Absence received them,
       personne: Keats saw some urn stolen

(the absence of Greece) a documentary urn
a hole in history, History of Art.
Remember Home?
When you would read your bright books

and listen through your parents' wall and listening
and reading were patterns of incomprehension.
There is a generation of boys
whose first glimpses of nude women were

the momentary horrors of newsreels, the liberations,
the flailing slender arms and flexible
breasts, the bodies
all shoveled into the open trench

military efficiency, medical need pouring them into
the ground. Concentration, and no one
to explain. No wonder
we are afraid, and Anne Frank's *true*

diary, her delicate dangerous adolescence revealed
in a book. History is full of shit.
The men we become
become the hideous enemy, the cold

erasure that shoved women into eternal naked
humiliation, on film. And they are not
humiliated, no one,
we are not. We thrill at the sight

of everyone's guilt, especially the neighbors'.
The world's a clear symptom, its music
and its birds a sign
of the silence that is possible, to anyone.

For I Have Already Been Once a Boy & a Girl, a Bush & a Bird, & a Leaping, Journeying Fish —Empedocles

Though his own existence is questioned, Leucippus is known to have said one thing: *Naught happens for nothing, but everything from a ground and of necessity*

I used to live where I longed for a life and all around me birds: *Ardea Occidentalis* that would come to my call and would eat fish from my boy's hand, dripping and ticklish. And the little blue heron, stalking his garden, ignoring me, angry at the capitulation of his cousin. None of this is true, but the air was blue and the water green. Tears were plentiful and credit available.

My mother spoke another language. My father wanted to know it too and would practice deep into the night. I would hear him beg her for lessons, and I heard her laugh in French. His family was German. They came from the swamps. They lived there, lives modest and constant.

There is too much to tell. Too little.

In my town Whites watched movies at "The Strand," Coloreds at "The Bengal." I had seen *Bengal Lancers* and envied the glamorous name of their building forbidden me. After it burned Negro children came to our balcony for Saturday matinees. Then the bus service ended for lack of demand, or because of events in Birmingham, and I no longer could get to the movies from our house in the country. I would play house. Often alone, sometimes with a girl who lived on our lane, sometimes under the real house cool and forbidden, sun glaring impotent all around as I arranged rooms and furnishings to sharpen a sense of place in the world, honing isolation into a shard gleaming in the dust. Sometimes the girl returned home unnoticed.

My mother spoke to herself taking shorthand. The fastest in the state, winner of all the prizes, and in her mind kept a record of everything except of birds. She hated birds and built a kind of cage in which we lived, we family of humans, clever.

I live the smallest lives from the movies.

When I prove small historic theorems from The Lives of the Particles, there is cleanliness and ambition for everyone.

There is water and mud and blurred edges. I love nautical sounds the ringing of chains on gunwales and the heavy rhythm of diesel. Not the sound of water, the sickening lapping. I like the rainbows of oil. The ringing

of anything but bells. Every boy reads too much

of the kind of scripture that comes on boxes, the shape of stenciling, of graffiti, of marks of lading, loading. India is out there. Temple bells sound like rigging. Wind of wide-screen oceans. The deadly threat of rust, all readable from shore, all the pagodas in China: tea and teasing, and waves by Hokusai. "A music which is like furniture."—Erik Satie

There's no bird brighter than the cardinal, no feather more astounding drifts from his startled rage. My mother loves the cardinal best, trails dozens from her skillful arms feeding.

I do not believe in the dead though I do feel sorry for them. I drove beyond the resort in the mountains and parked on the pavement. After a time the engine stopped ticking and the Milky Way bore intensely down, but the sound of air thickening in the cold and the complaint of insects frightened me home. I had seen the sharp peaks of Maroon Bells against starlight.

A man I knew said amazement is not knowledge. For instance, people do bad things to each during history, good intentions bowing on the hillside, daffodils, like the dead. All those children in the dark breath above us, watching cowboys ambushed by each other while ranches glow in the distance under the starlight in Colorado. It all fits, and the future is no more surprising than the past.

And the Light Never Waned in the Same Way Twice

> For it was not until the body was appeased that he could come alive in his mind. . . . And life in his mind gave him pleasure, such pleasure that pleasure was not the word.—Samuel Beckett

Another life or something she can see
Far into, like a future, some other form
Of failure. Wanting to waste into beauty
She ate little and loved the air like flesh

Third person, as much a part of any self as
Isolation, home or some other
Place in the mountains, something fast
Or if not the mountains the seaside, or

The shore like sanded loam of some sere
Suburban garden where anything is other;
There is no denying weather when in morning
Mist or yellow light lifts

Its skirt slightly to step across the glitter:
Green as the map on a wall
Bristling little pins in colors, its litter.
And beneath that a potted plant

Postcard landscape, a rock; all arranged
A dream come. True, we are
Better than we'd hoped to be, in a way:
But still not good enough or thin.

It is so sad, it is morning. To the cynical all
Is theory after all. And there are
Birds in the air. And in the tree enthralled
They sing to each other,

You must admit, not to you.
Who was she? Casting no shadow
Sidling to the future in that meadow
Teratogenic mammals graze.

There's a kind of bird that crowds
Into a garden raucously.
We choose to call it *song*, endowed
As we are with a nervous past.

She slenderly floats down the ruined stair.
Some fun. Ruin. A fluoroscope,
The future shows like ribs, laddered bare
Glittering. Feed her ghastly hope

The Romantic ruin I saw near the beach
On the Atlantic, an island heavily honed
By hurricanes, pierced by palms and each
Oak draped in epiphytic bromeliads heavy

With arrogance: strong men lived there
During centuries never more beautiful
Than now, not less thin, skeletal, where
Anyone could know the wind wafting full

Of every authority. Or did you know me then
When I was thinning into art, my poem of self
As if I could, too, dance . . . I could slowly thin
Into laughter, if I wanted, if I cared. (Slender

Among his rocks he walks the paths trees
A garden quibbles behind his back.
Love the large, she advised, which bite like fleas
And words. His random routes

Through the mountains his souvenirs,
Stones to make garden paths. He rolled rocks into
His car, along the highway stones were
Insolent with lichen, arrogant with ontology,

A splash of interest among jettisoned junk.
Late in the year tree bark oozes a kind of tear,
(Disease among the spruce), like sound,
Faint aromas of long evenings and short memories.

Something large, she said, attach to, considerable
Other. Inside or out, fear something big. So home
He wanders quiet among his minerals,
Politest among men and dogs. (History is a whore,

Said Shostakovich. And a certain blind
Man hated birds, his sore
Eyes blind from birth, he, geometer of sound,
Never saw birds' habits or colors.

A blind man's love of history bound
Him to his bed while his sister read
To him books all through the night her voice ground
Into gravel pity for a brother. History's

More boring than music, less kind.) Among his rocks
He walks the paths of his garden, trees
Surround him and words quibble behind his back.
Love the big, she advised, which bites like the flea.

There is room here for some nostalgia (*sun perch*,
sun porch), tormenting like the last remaining cat,
Tormenting like the cat the last remaining rat,
Tormenting like the green eyes of potatoes

In the cellar reaching for what light,
What used to be called, *light*.) I knew such a word.
Pale flesh remembers the bruise in spite
Of the ill-fitting noose, the freedom allowed.

Pale flesh and torn. Remembering to suffer but lacking
Ardor, such a childhood, all full of future,
Is nevertheless beautiful and fills the mind as if
With momentary stars, or scars. Never less.

After school, when the world thrusts
Itself from geography, history, algebra—into music—
There's a kind of person who—who trusts
The social order. Has faith, for instance: Shoots up

In an alley, sleeps drunk in the subway, talks
Back to Mom. Crowds of starlings take
Shape this way, forming and reforming against the sunset a
Flourish. In the forest. Make

A flourish sadder than the young humans do.
Eye to brain to spine. Men do this, and boys, they look
At glistening flesh, and the abstraction of hair
Mingled with air, wave, waving there.

Life works this way in the city: cutting through crowds
Of flesh the boys and men and women cling
To themselves thinking they touch, loudly
Thinking they are an edge, a boundary

Burning with will. Still they sell
And buy and belong to each other.
So lovely a lie they tell, well
Accustomed to the little ways, of flesh,

The simplicity. (Nothing in nature is sadder
Than children swirling to music.) Dance.
The subject returns to the mad or
The merely angry, the difference between

Talking and not. Holding hands.
Speech and silence. So then I remembered
The sounds of tempered steel falling on sand,
And the mimetic vibrations: musical.

Telephone lines,
    plucked by wind
Gorgeously. There was weather and power, a day of diminution
Among the mountains, the enormous deciduous climbing their
    flanks —
no,
Evergreens, the only immortality in cold and thin air. Here
Where I live, Love,

Longing turns crystalline sometimes in evening the sky
Alight with letters, long strings and square arrays, matrices
And this a kind of fond delusion:
That everyone is always in every way wrong, although
Not just a few of us will live long enough
To despair at last among the conspiring molecules
Tremulous again in sunlight, the trees
The swirling conceit
    of the mortal all
Resolved to fill the moments.

I used to remember the little fish we would catch,
its name. And the deep anger
of the afternoon returning with dust and fish.
One would have thought it odd to live otherwise,
but one would have grasped for alternative, *a word*
if not a wisdom. And the nights are beyond me, you know,
those nights painted on velvet, gaudy beyond reason.
And the stars were not numberless, merely pointless.

How Light Is Spent

Two half-brothers fully blind
living together
a historian and a piano player.
Neither cared for birds,
cacophonous,
birds. Both uncles
blind from birth.

Half my uncles' days
no darker than any child's sleep but the sounds
that came, their one talent listening, through
thin walls were death to hide:

distraction being
the better part of valor after spring
thaw the forsythia bend
graceful above
pools admiring their own linear
progression.

The vanity of the blind manifests
in a soul more bent to serve to present
its true account—or returning the soul
returning like a vampire in the morning
to darkness after dark

                                        day labor light
denied. The two blind uncles would
walk with new girlfriends in the spring park
down prim paths patient
to prevent the murmurs

but children would giggle
like tinfoil as they passed
children would glitter hysterical

                        as they kissed.
Bearing the mildest yoke of a little lust
blind uncles walked home
to an apartment shared
like kingly state. Spring birds blared
from skies but blind uncles passed them by.

                        Thousands speed
.   without rest but two blind uncles for dinner
stand caressing peas on a plate
at three o'clock,
mashed potatoes at nine, the plate a clock face,
a form of knowledge like sight.
Before bed then
to stare through any wall

                        at this dark world and
wide. And the reading of bedtime stories
the outdoing of one's self undoing partial
life a knotted fall of yarn ambitious to be
a sweater. The felt life. The history
of the dark is the music of sleep.

Toying

To be alone and afraid.
Or to listen intently while staring
through walls. Or the world
wanders aimless generally
toward *future* as mist
gathers on the window
veined meanders, a glitter.

Anyone can change the world.

Desire was a popular word. They
would say it with a wink (some
called it a leer) with certain sharp
gestures, arabesques waist high.
It drains like blood from the classroom.

When I was young we counted
the enemy dead daily in the papers.
A small race who spoke a pagan language.
They were French, which was odd, but the world
contains itself with a certain clarity,
a wholeness, and a touching belief
in the future. We children chanted

in hallways and would not go to class.
We burned flags and little cards
and looked desirous at the neighbor.
Her skin was as alabaster, as if
blood were a faint glow, a lamp,

a warmth and a light, her tongue
burned a beacon in the dark cloud
of her speech. *Rally*. All
speech is prayer.

We Children were frightened and sparks
sprayed down around us burning
our little umbrellas. We laughed.
We would eagerly read the papers,
loving the shapes of the letters, longing
for the brave shapes of our toys.

Toy Houses in the Landscape

Shrines, temples, grottoes, or
a little house on the altar complete
with curtains and a key (livery of seisen)
on a chain, the right- and left-hand apses
each a quiet house for a favored saint;
faith and fantasy.

Censorious. Sacred smell arises
from the hand of the old priest
the little altar boy also serves
and waits, stands then
kneels thinking sacred or
profane thoughts. Fantasies.

from *The Tao of Painting*: Method of
Painting Clouds in *hsi kou* outline style:
clouds are the ornaments of sky and earth,
the embroidery of mountains and streams.
. . . in the emptiness of clouds there are
no traces of brushwork . . .

I sat next to a thin lake where trees
and grasses yellowed. The rare jogger
and walking couples would pass,
the lapping of tiny waves and the ravens
and crows, no smaller birds, would
only to their own kind call;

for thirty years I have carried these lines,
for no reason my little Latin: *Passer, deliciae meae*
puellae, quicum ludere, quem in sinu tenere
unhappy Catullus and me brooding
on girls, on birds,
small sentimental failures.

At the end of autumn and
at the beginning of spring willows
that look as though they had been cropped
should be painted against bamboo fences
and near hamlets; they are like a young
girl whose hair has been trimmed . . .

Beyond measure and full of promise
a swallow or chimney swift
rises on its own exuberance
a bird of free will like a Spy
or Heroick Villain, Bird of
the Birds, A Boy Among

Boys—oh never again
pronounce the word
(O God make us children
of quietness and heirs of peace
said Clement, Bishop of Rome.
Let Cherub rejoice with Cherub

who is a bird and a blessed Angel
said Christopher Smart) say the word
Angel. Some of the words
begin to be true, like a beam of light
through the smoke at the movies
midair and theatrical.

Affection if not
face: the clear-eyed years beyond her
too late this child looked at Mondrian
his clear ideas
at white squares and yellow rectangles
blue squares with

black clean lines caressing.
She moved to peer into the face of Corot's
Woman in Thought Eighteen Fifty-Five
her past her pathos my sweet
alyssum and foxglove, my garden
in the shade in summer and summer ends

this way hosta and cimicifuga and
Japanese painted fern.
The first cold nights of fall I avert
my eyes from the visible breath of women
passing, so shameful an intimacy.
In landscape paintings, in addition

to scenery there should be figures (*jên*)
and other living things (*wu*). They
should be drawn well and with style,
though not in too great detail.
One must live in longing and suffer
only a little toward evening.

Crisis

Respond to me, my unknown,
I am searching for you!—Anna Akhmatova, 1913

It was during those days when you could still walk alone
down railroad tracks and across the creosoted trestles
if you felt no vibrations through the track and the sun was setting
you could watch, and then keep walking counting your steps.
Someone began to walk along and spoke to me of the future
and there was no danger and there was a little laughter.
A stranger as in the Bible. We walked in the night then turned
each a different way and I went to my house and grew up
and lived a life. And people who meant no harm
have suffered.

Aristotle said that gravity is the quality of material things
that causes them to move downward, levity the quality
of material things that causes them to rise. A balance
between the two, as with, for instance, air, would cause them
to hover. Aristotle was often wrong, as when he counted teeth.
Still, the words work. *Gravity* is such a lovely nexus:
seriousness, sadness, and the tendency of things to huddle—
such as a family in crisis or hikers in high country. *Levity*
is less useful, having descended in contemporary usage
to playfulness, although still related to leverage, to forcefulness
and odd sorts of alleviations.

One delight of childhood was the View-master, the binocular
device for three-dimensional viewing; you held it to your eyes
and pulled a sort of trigger on the side and you floated through
the eyes into the depth of the scene before you. The makers
of stereopticons, magic lanterns, stereoscopes, and View-masters

delight in travelogues, deep or wide
places with vistas, with framing oaks and long corridors
of fastigiate pines and balsamic firs.

My favorite emotion was sadness. Nothing grand, the small
domestic sense of limitation and loss. Between the comic mask
and the tragic there is a straight-line mouth of the merely sad.
Somber but not sullen. Sexy? Equilibrium amidst
the flurries of mania and depression.

Uncle Diedrich would grasp my right hand, a handshake,
and with his left hand knead my right shoulder, and I could feel
information flow through that connection. He not only knew
I was unforgivably thin and weak, but he knew why. I felt
his Braille-trained fingers extract all my secrets and while
his vague smile told me he would not expose me, would keep
all he knew to himself, it was still a humiliation. I learned
to avoid touch, developed techniques to avoid that electrical
danger. This is why the floating world of the blind
so disturbs the sighted, you
gravely attached to your fulcrum of light.

Famous Poems of the Past Explained

Imagine how much I hope, imagine
what a fan I am, how I want to read
wisdom, yes, and applaud such confidence.
I was about to step when I noticed
there was no world there, so I turned
quickly searching for foot-sized solidity
to enhance my belief in the future.
Then I noticed the little yellow flowers
that sprang timely in my footprints

impressions graceful and slender as a past.
Another time you were with me and we
were young it had to do with sex
we breathed heavily the hard air
and saw our own internal shapes turn white
in front of us then fade into the borrowed
dusk of the room. It was perhaps
our first time, and I was in love
with your bravery, how you fearlessly

gave yourself into yourself, so I gathered
a small nosegay of yellow violets
that were the color of the bed
and of the dust floating languorous.
And then the barest small foot of you
kept creeping into my memory, as if
I had seen you naked and unafraid, as
each tiny foot of yours impressed itself
in the snow and the white nativity

of the season turned itself sorrowful
but so attractively. No one knew better
than you the look of the afternoon,
and how the foot is slim and of a shape
to win a woman's greatest ease and note that
the memory fades, and I pay my bill
and walk home past the flower shops.
Orpheus tracing his steps back to the surface
to make music again; how the instrument

is a body of wood breathing, a wisdom of
will and carpentry given voice; how he knew
tunes to turn trees into audience. Anyway,
the little family in the church held their dirty hymnals
and sang the old songs to the wheezing
box behind them. Nobody thought about anything
much: hunger, horror, the grand harmonies
of the light, the night where nothing
but blossoms of stars would crowd

and tumultuous clouds come pouring
over the rim from Canada
tendering the shiny coin of rain upon the plain:
Let not the darke thee cumber;
What though the Moon do's slumber?
         the starres of the night
         will lend thee their light,
like Tapers cleare without number.

                                        —for Linda

Testimony

DANIEL

16   And I have heard of thee, that thou canst make interpretations, and dissolve doubts: now if thou canst read the writing, and make known to me the interpretation thereof, thou shalt be clothed with scarlet, and have a chain of gold about thy neck, and shalt be the third ruler in the kingdom.

17   Then Daniel answered and said before the king, Let thy gifts be to thyself, and give thy rewards to another; yet I will read the writing unto the king, and make known to him the interpretation.

It starts with new names imposed upon the defeated. And who chose his own name anyway? Not me. Or maybe me, sort of. At least Daniel is recalled by his Israelite name, not like Shadrach, Meschach, Abednego. Anyway here was Daniel, doing a little dream analysis, a little psychologizing, and here we are again, full of woe and wariness. I like this one because he stands here surrounded by languages and cultures not his own, and he reads to save his life and he sleeps through the night while the king keeps dreaming dreams and suffering.

And remember the music? *The sound of the cornet, flute, harp, sackbut, psaltery, dulcimer, and all kinds of musick.* And the feet of clay. And *The sound of the cornet, flute, harp, sackbut, psaltery, dulcimer, and all kinds of musick*

They'll give you a slave name when you're not wary. Finding your name is hard science, and who can you believe, Mom?

the examined life is unlivable

to entice you   *nothing is bigger*
closer   *than the night,*
     here *enormous and warm*
near the mountains the   *or cold*
    sun swerves hopeless

into evening
    birds waver

some minor form of future

    gleams seductive
      a handful of shards:

       "... and   *we live*
  when we touch, small   *this way, full*
  sparks of inertia   *of all possible*
  will into the night sky fly *pasts*
  so pretty, so ordinary"

when he was working
Matisse believed in God
but everyone takes a holiday

  on this earth,
    the author of a faithless agony,
the god of smaller animals—today is his minor holiday
      and sparrows know his name

sadness, dangerous
    as the habits of birds:
I've loved it too much but will now
    grow like a treefull of serendipitous
birds O happy birds

18   Then the king went to his palace, and passed the night fasting: neither were instruments of musick brought before him: and his sleep went from him.
19   Then the king arose very early in the morning, and went in haste unto the den of lions.

    anyway it is possible to live
    tending a garden mornings moving higher
    during the rainy season just in case keeping
    a diary riding like a dog in a pickup the long
they wear   afternoon into sleep
music in
their ears   and you can call it happiness if you want

    men and women wander past each other in the night they
    are young and love to dance they dream awake they
    wear music in their ears they dance with anything they
    keep up their strength they drink coffee they dance they
    don't ever stop they wander past each other it is morning

It is night and I am listening to music. I am alone and listening to music. Is this cause for joy or for despair? This small machine I manage gives me a power beyond Count von Walsegg's, and I am still alone in spite of music. (Oh so what.) The sounds come pouring into the room out of two small boxes. Some people keep it out of the room, allow a boiling directly into their ears, a hissing can be heard in line at the theater, or as they pass jogging in the streets. Or in their cars the bass dominant the very trees along the highways throb to that beat like a comet passing too near.

In the night the dead Shostakovich.
My dead uncle. You had one, too, no doubt, you who are not here to read this over my shoulder. My uncle made music as best he could. He died and I think about him without grief and I worry at my loss of grief. Once I grieved but I no longer grieve. Is it a fault? My uncle told stories of the Merchant Marine, and he read stories of ships and such, of The War and of the scattered peace that never followed him. He as out of place as any child in his own childhood. All my uncles smoked pipes. All my aunts were saints or schoolteachers. My mother is still alive.

In the night my mother weeps for her sisters, all suffering. Who does not?

Chemistry is the sacred text, the richest manipulation like music. All art aspires to the condition of chemistry. Valences and variations. What is sweeter than the long rows of symbols and the quaint turns of phrase, the jars and tubes and tabulations. I want to know a thing and did love a person or two as fully as this, would know them if I could their fullness of purpose and paradox.

    What is worth discovering is for instance tiny
    and crystalline in structure, of the allotropic form
    consisting entirely of carbon and hydrogen—no,

but something impossible anyway. How can I tell
you? I want the pieces to fit, bright and dark.

You can make almost anything with a little carbon
and a little hydrogen. Maybe some oxygen. It's
that kind of world. Still, it is dark out there
and the music continues from this box: I imagine
your face as you slightly bored listen but politely.

Maybe we'll need nitrogen, too.

And yet

ché non è impresa da pigliare a gabbo
discriver fondo a tutto l'universo,
né da lingua che chiami mamma or babbo.

                    Inferno, canto xxxii
it is not a job to take lightly
to describe the basis of the universe,
not for the tongue that cries "mama" or "papa"

                    I am, as they say,
a dying animal, no more,
I will number the stripes of the lily.
I want to know what everything looks like,
like the only passion left, the single emotion.

Why do I not remember my dreams? Do you?
(I hate wisdom most, fear it—my only advice
to you is: avoid the Wise, they sow wickedness
where they least intend, and even when they
are sorry, so what?—I learned this in my sleep)

the sun's on the other side of the planet bothering the birds
while over here, now, this very moment, as my machine
pumps symphonically, the birds blissfully dream their bird
    dreams
into the tiny warmth of their smooth breathing—
a bird breathing into the night air, the swirl
the dynamic flow, the molecular disturbance, the little birds
blameless in the dark and doomed

    the sun delirious in its design
dark, elsewhere
swooning

my music flutters into the air
the dark, like light would
the sound of the light
the weight of the music rising
the simple molecules happy as anyone
examining their collective conscience finding all is well.

AMNESIA

15 I Daniel was grieved in my spirit in the midst of my body,
and the visions of my head troubled me.

We made a sad parade into the roadside restaurant
no words   to mind I
watched her face   empty
itself

Se tendió la vaca herida (Lorca)
a child in the corner sharpened

his knife and hunger
waiting for the cow to die

she tries to recall   names her
wounded memory throbs   with
the name of the child in the corner

not if her life   it remember
depended on   we drank wine
                           the color of

it   remember
we drank wine
the color of   light fleeing

(a child milked a cow each   morning
and leaned his head   leaned against

and felt her breath and heard the grinding teeth
and heard the din of milk in the bucket
the boy in the corner has no   name)

the land darkened
because the moon had gone:
the horns of a cow one kind of danger

memory another wine
the color of
light every month arriving   phases of shadow

long
and lovely the way out and   who could blame her?

her memory of the eager
boy the balanced   boy eager
enough to touch

and me? I see it, don't worry
weather happens   and the light
so when she stands against

the light her dress   and draperies
diaphanous
someone tell the neighbors
someone drink to her life   in light.

(or this as the only story —   we ride
like the skier the avalanche   — the explosion. Big
Bang. Long time, ago,   we are, you are the blast itself
: we ride like snowmen an
avalanche, and try to not fall. There is no end)   sunset:
at the very moment
of the light going the color deepens   *beyond bearing,*
will touch you with such —   *you can feel*
nothing but your own future   *collapsing sweetly.*
Do you choose

new world symphonies

6:7   Therefore at that time, when all the people heard the sound of
the cornet, flute, harp, sackbut, psaltery, and all kinds of musick, all
the people, the nations, and the languages, fell down and worshipped
the golden image that Nebuchadnezzar the king had set up.

speech over silence?
To move from nothing to something the once
vanishingly small universe infinitely dense

mere
absence widens the meshes to include as much of nothing as
gravity will allow.

I waited for her at the one restaurant in this corner of Wyoming
while the wind of Wyoming tore the points off pennants
little bright plastic flags to attract the attention of us travelers
        hungry and
thirsty who would stand and listen
                while a flag roared protesting against molecules
particles
a flag its absolute sound tearing itself to tatters selvage
and there was a moon and everything nothing missing. We
        were traveling together and she worried

Memory is kind, a kindness, a kind of unlistening, a gray wall
        even
toward which you move. (Michael Palmer said this)

She was hitchhiking or she was my mother
along the road and the landscape withered where she stepped
the long landscape unrolled scrolling

itself independent of her or me I stopped
and she rode alongside me it became Wyoming
after Colorado was she my sister?
I have known landscapes
the cows tend to all face the same
direction
the wind withers us all

silence

        she forgot
to speak to me as the landscape lapsed

the color of
the tender emptiness   lying
the dust her most becoming
color and under the moon
a shadow of earth stalking the moon

she rode with me   as a child I grew
a kind of flower   it felt like straw
muted color   my flower my mother
gave me seeds each spring and I grew
a small bed of them I did not love them
I remember them   not the name
their languor their listless need

here is where it gets beautiful
she has a photograph   of real children
she has a photograph   of a dog
she has a photograph   of a kind of man
blurred about the edges

a railroad follows the roadway for twenty miles a hundred
parallel lines   the axiom of parallels is not always
   true
conic sections open along the roadway   home

Satie is easy to play she says   her hands twitch   this
is a clue   a piano is furniture   she says
her face twitches   each note shines separate   she
says   the radio crackles across Wyoming her   face
shines in the setting sun   Satie knew a thing
she says   she nods to no one

and when the day began to wear away, then came the twelve,
and said unto him, Send the multitude away, that they may go
into the towns and country round about, and lodge, and get
victuals: for we are here in a desert place. Luke 9:12

Deserts breed religion   she said   her face twitched
Zion, this is the place   her hands formed *Sonatine*
   bureaucratique
in the air   *je te veux*   *Poudre d'or*   crazies live here
she said to me sitting   traveling at seventy miles per hour
across Wyoming   she began to sing

to hunger to thirst
the moon rose to our left   it crossed as if
the moon mattered
the desert is my home she said

                                        no more
the horns of a crescent moon a trick of light
we all live here   the cows of Wyoming remember

Se tendió la vaca herida
a child in the corner sharpens

his knife and hunger
waiting for the cow to die

she tries to recall   names her
wounded memory throbs   with
the name of the child

in the corner as

if her life   it
depended on
                   the color
of the eclipse.

28   Hitherto is the end of the matter. As for me Daniel, my
cogitations much troubled me, and my countenance changed in me,
but I kept the matter in my heart.

The little boys and girls in rows see the hand moving and the gray
wall and who can interpret the writing there? the teacher asks. The
hand writing on the wall, the blackboard in musical chalk, the ear-
destroying screech of knowledge called wisdom called down even
unto how many generations and who didn't hate it. A teacher in
white linen who knows how to read will teach you if you suffer
enough—I said to her when she corrected me, "My judge is God,"
and she failed to see the humor there but then we were some of us
happy in our little hearts I suppose riding the yellow bus home
knowing we soon would but we would have to remember, memory
the burden memory the vulnerability, ultimately read the secrets of
the world at the end of school days.

Wast ever in court, shepherd? No, truly.
Then thou art damned

what can you do with a boy who wants the world beautiful who
would kill to make it so you must be careful with him yes kiss
him make him well notice the rain redeeming itself on your roof
the proof theological there the ambiguous there is a last rose in
that garden this fall dreary among the welter of leaves the
arrogance wearying talk me into it he said threatening love each
the other but we are no longer ancient in a narrow bed and we
know some thing or two——, compared to pain everyone knows
pain but we were young together going to the park with wine
then the rain drove us home where we opened our bottle and
across the roofs of New Orleans we watched the gray rain fall
pretend we knew a hunger for weather dismal that afternoon
and dreary and gray the passing and it is a coming into one's
own entering even the language like elephants into Italy no alp
too high all trumpet and splash (the flame of the match becomes
the flame of the candle (or the split amoeba becomes only itself
forever) even if the match lies dead on the carpet or *Bungalow*
and *Bengali* as words curious to the English ear confused but
then Herodotus spoke of the aptness of belief ears less than eyes
the body being full of fun and mystery——*Mimosa* was one of my
favorites the word the tree left a mess after rain on the sidewalk
as of writing grapheme delicate pink soon decayed to ink I read
that in a book—— I looked up from a book me reading in the
mountains toward the double rainbow one of many in these
mountains during this summer and there is no rainbow only in
the reader's mind the eye's trick mythic as any mirroring ear is
heir to——that place below the throat that delicate indentation
beloved by the hero of the novel of his beloved's body when it

mattered matter and the body the coming into one's own.) "Safe
with my lynxes, feeding grapes to my leopards," Pound wrote the
man wrote early in a long dangerous career careening path (the
French for *quarry* as in hunt or stone) translation is hard
(*crossroad* career *carrière*) the French for anything in his small
memory of Mom and you'd think he'd grow up by now a life
"And I worship I have seen what I have seen" he knew so much
and hated so many he was sad as all get out at the end he ended
that way famous the cantos "And the frogs singing against the
fauns in the half-light. And . . ." So I was only eight years old and
the night before the trip I was saddened knowing now the trip
was upon me it was soon to be over and this excess of anticipation
ruled my remaining life the next night on the barge I smelled
the lettuce, bananas hung from the rafters near my sleeping-
cabin and the water below me indifferently brown crawled across
to the Gulf to an ocean and the water below me crawled across
the mud and the dead man and the detritus of where we lived in
time of where I spent that summer anticipating the dismal
ending the return to land and frogs singing I would remember
forever the lights on the river and the indifferent curl of wake as
the great ships passed our grocery barge where we would sell to
sailors food and they would sometimes tell us stories and they
loved to tell us stories and at night the smell of lettuce and
bananas became stories to sell and in the dark the ships' bells
would hover and all of this in America even though sailors were
Greek and Russian and full of all anger the river full of America
swirling dangerous and brown full of wake but day doth daily
draw my sorrows longer And night doth nightly make grief's
strength seem stronger he said when it was necessary he looked
further into the night then turned to his companion and looked
further into the night and turned beyond that last corner turned
tightly inward as the owls called as owls will to some relative or
against the random darkness, which is never perfect and anyway

is filled with the scratching of little feet clawed and clever of
endangered rodents still the man and woman turn toward each
other in the night who can ever forget such a moment such
random moments that make a couple of lives pathetic "Mr Pitt
said that wd / surprise people here for that wars never interrupted
the interest of DEBTS Fat of the spermaceti whale gives the
clearest and most beautiful light of any substance known in
nature" nice nature in the Cantos argue against us all and the
words continue to expand like any universe there is nothing to
be done nothing beautiful but still the boy lingers in the night
and thinks the stars might do and thinks the moon might do
and thinks the streetlight might do and thinks the taillights
disappearing redly into the horizon the line where sky but listen
Rilke is still alive no but his friend Balthus is still alive and they
talked one to the other as the stars were heaving their little lights
out into the clueless nights and they learned stuff and in the eye
of one of them the eye of a panther continued to not blink as if
he really saw a panther in a zoo and the image, which is after all
mere light and that itself a matter of dance vibrations dance is
nothing descend into the matter of the beast dark-skinned beast
and they spoke into the night as if no one was listening as the
stars shed their skins into the universe great shells of dancing
particles hurtling madly into our eyes yours and mine so Pound
never spoke to me I would not have liked him too cruel who
walked with a stick and banged boys' shins I bet who threw rocks
his way and bottles and Italy kept him what did they know his
Italian better than his Chinese still I wish I had known some
Epic Poet who was alive as if you could tell the difference long
they talk into the night who listens as the crickets or local variety
of noisome insect no no not mephitic noisy is all we meant insects
kept their rhythms because they cannot help it any old man's ears
will hear see them any two talking in the dark lost "and those
negroes by the clothes-line are extraordinarily / like the figures

del Cossa Their green does not swear at the landscape 2 months'
life in 4 colours ter flediliter: Ityn to close the temple of Janus
bifronte the two-faced bastard 'and the economic war has begun'"
crazy about money he was against it and crazy us we know better
we are perfect money in my youth God loved the poor and we
gave coins with faces on one side and birds on the other and now
the poor are evil you know it anyone can see it in their eyes we
don't like failure anyone the insects the dogs and they are lazy
that's the reason my uncle who could barely read he worked and
built his own house of trash cast off particle board isn't it pretty
to think so my uncle did not like to work either like an artist or
philosopher but loved his coffee and the shade it was the south
where shade is an art the mellifluous chatter of photons will burn
blisters into the pavement the poor live in the shade where there
are a few coins remaining with faces of Roman emperors and
whores women who had money from love never in the sunlight
where it burns "and the economic war has begun" the man said
and he called it a poem an epic I was happy to be alone in those
days and would walk down railroad tracks because there were
not many left and the rails were often rusted think of it the
weight of the trains how they shined the rails and at dusk you
could see them for miles the lingering rails glittering redly on
their ties to walk was odd the distance between ties unnatural a
curious dance as the insects hopped across at your feet you had to
keep your eyes down or risk stepping on sharp stones ballast the
round earth moving under your feet the sun as round as anything
from a distance and red think of running here and jumping into
an open car the power at your feet the railroad fortunes and
pointless men jumping on at will at whim sometimes they fell
under the crushing wheels juggernaut oh well and some had
families states and counties distant who I guess never found out
and still the power to just jump on anybody's train when curves
slow them down that was the life those were the days my uncle

had a job and everyboy can work now the unions are going with
the railroads but look at the chicory growing there more blue and
tolerant than the eyes of any democrat a kind woman once spoke
to me she said important things and books could be written and
there are things to do important things to do I was walking in
the dust along the road happy or not it is not important was I
happy? Perhaps I was happy she gave me a ride it was summer it
was always summer in those years and the dust gave a sense of
delirium to the view the view the horizons were prepared in all
directions I was far from home by foot but not so far in time she
gave me a ride she was kind this was long ago and the world was
only itself she asked for nothing more than I would gladly give
later when the look of those little blue flowers had faded she said
it would make me immortal she was right so far still not such a
gift as one might hope will not pay the rent won't make anyone
happy you can read about it we were always happy when we
thought about we lived that way loving everyone and knowing
how to read Greek for instance or Latin we were better at Latin
but Greek was good for something special and private I mean the
old Greek only the old politics about and beyond the Then
Leucothea had pity, "mortal once Who now is a sea-god: *νόστου*
γαίης Φαιήχων, . . ." "What? (Cantos, 95) can it mean can it
matter? Anything can she taught me that or someone did
. . . *Odysseus was swept overboard by a huge wave, and the rich*
robes which he wore dragged him down to the sea-depths until his
lungs seemed about to burst. Yet being a powerful swimmer, he
managed to divest himself of the robes, regain the surface, and
scramble back on the raft. The pitiful goddess Leucothea, formerly
Ino, wife of Athamas, alighted beside him there, disguised as a
seamew. In her beak she carried a veil, which she told Odysseus to
wind around his middle before plunging into the sea again. This
veil would save him, she promised—Robert Graves   . . . *till*
inundation rise Above the highest Hills: then shall this Mount Of

Paradise by might of Waves be moovd Out of his place, pushd by
the horned floud, With all his verdure spoil'd, and Trees adrift
Down the great River to the op'ning Gulf, And there take root an
Iland salt and bare, The haunt of Seales and Orcs, and Sea-mews
clang. To teach thee that god attributes to place No sanctitie, if
none be thither brought by Men who there frequent, or therein
dwell—John Milton   it is a kind of seagull a white bird happy
above the waves nothing more Have you been saved? awkward
silence awkward salvation at best silence you have a connection to
the kosmos she would say and something smaller than that
something domestic she spoke to him as she cooked she cradled
the telephone he pictured this in that place surrounded by
warmth that place near the throat and cradling shoulder where
a child's face would peer at you as you walked behind the young
mother whose useful body so intrigued you turned you into
something less dangerous less full of the dailiness and anyway
she spoke to me as she blanched the greens and heated oil and I
could hear a knife slice onion and as the imagined molecules
formed she said Have you been saved? and I said Many times and
here is room for more these dangers of the domestic these
maternal moments make me weep ashamedly in the privacy of
my own telephone booth hard it is and how full of fury to be
saved to be salvageable it is a kind of decorum it is necessary in
the strictest sense Anyone can weep can cry real tears it is a trick
too easy I believe in everything everything but nothing can save
such unbelief some bird some passion for air or light or maybe it
is god in that form makes sense withering into light withering
like the state slender as the wind particles pared to feathers and
fierce-eyed flight god in the arrogant air catching a current
riding the thermals that's me or should be a dove a docile form of
pigeon short-lived but then she turned to me her lips on the
receiver she turned as if I were over her shoulder waiting she
smiled into the air the electrons and the little family's dinner

hissed think of it of flight and the feather tips bending with the
weave of wind seamews ride behind the garbage scows filling the
air and weak minds with screams delirious with desire fulfilled
filling their sweetening bodies with rotting residue of whose life
mine egg shells parings grease of what small animals the dead
and decomposing of the city followed by the glittery gulls see
them against a sunset let's say why not a touch of romance a
salvation god gathering likely ambiguities into her mouth sharp
beaked and belligerent a man a woman encopulant watch all
from their bed the room for rent and nothing is more beautiful
nothing less than saved by all bright gods and tiny temptations
save all give us this day our daily bread and forgive us but day
doth daily draw my sorrows longer and night doth nightly make
grief's strength seem stronger make it new pretend she sings to
you pretend she sings to you she flies to you pretend she flies to
you she sings she dances you need not pretend god dances with
you she takes your hand oh pretend and nothing is more
beautiful nothing less saved by the bright brittle gods their tiny
temptations

Notes

"Chivalric": *Knights Baronets* defined in *Brewer's Dictionary of Phrase and Fable: Classic Edition, Giving the Derivation, Source, or Origin of Common Phrases, Allusions and Words that Have a Tale to Tell* (Blitz Editions: London, 1990).

"Enter Celia, with a Writing": René Char, *"Les Matinaux, Qu'il Vive!"*

"A History of Tenderness": *"Personne,* That's French for nobody — and also means somebody, just to confuse you students of French. I'm an orphan, a widower, an exile, a monk" from William Wiser, *The Circle Tour* (Atheneum: New York, 1988). Alan Dugan, "Lament for Cellists and Jacqueline Dupré," from *Poems Six* (Ecco Press: New York, 1989). Bruno Latour, "Irreductions," from *The Pasteurization of France*, translated by Alan Sheridan and John Law (Harvard University Press: Cambridge, 1988). Wallace Stevens, "Comme Dieu dispense de Graces," pt. 5 of "Poems from 'Lettres d'un Soldat,'" from *Opus Posthumous* (Random House: New York, 1957). Pablo Casals describing his reaction to first hearing a cello. Holly Stevens would not allow her picture to be taken, but I did not know this. At dinner I borrowed a Polaroid camera to commemorate the event, pushed the button, but as she was angrily explaining to me her aversion, the instant photograph I had taken of Ms. Stevens turned completely black.

"And the Light Never Waned in the Same Way Twice": the title is taken from Samuel Beckett. For Beth Nugent, whose *Live Girls* (Knopf, 1996) inspired the best parts of this poem.

"How Light Is Spent": Milton's Sonnet XIX.

Regarding the three "Toy" poems: "Once it accommodates evil (by which I mean / change, others, time) the toy becomes art," from "Looking into the Boxes of Joseph Cornell" by Richard Howard.

"Toy Houses in the Landscape": see Chieh Tzu Yuan Hua Chuan (1679–1701), *The Mustard Seed Garden Manual of Painting*, translated by Mai-Mai Sze (Bollingen Series, Princeton University Press, 1956). Clear-eyed years = clear ideas. For Wayne Dodd.

"Famous Poems of the Past Explained": Robert Herrick's "The Night-piece, to Julia."

"Testimony":

Daniel (whose name means *My Judge is God*), warns of what will happen at *kaytz ha-yomin*, the end of days, and speaks to an angel dressed in white linen, among other adventures.

As You Like It: III, ii.

"French for quarry": with gratitude to Caryl Lloyd:

J'ai de l'education.

"Vous voilà armé pour la lutte—a fait mon professeur en me disant adieu.—Qui triomphe au collège entre en vainqueur dans la carrière."

Quelle carrière?

Un ancien camarade de mon père, qui passait à Nantes, et est venu lui rendre visite, lui a raconté qu'un de leurs condisciples d'autrefois, un de ceux qui avaient eu tous les prix, avait été trouvé mort, fracassé et sanglant, au fond d'une carrière de pierre, où il s'était jeté après être resté trois jours sans pain.

—Jules Vallès, *Le bachelier* (1881)

Shakespeare, Sonnet 28.

Robert Graves, *The Greek Myths* (Penguin, 1955), 170, y.

Milton, *Paradise Lost*, Book XI.

The Iowa Poetry Prize and
Edwin Ford Piper Poetry Award Winners

1987

Elton Glaser, *Tropical Depressions*

Michael Pettit, *Cardinal Points*

1988

Bill Knott, *Outremer*

Mary Ruefle, *The Adamant*

1989

Conrad Hilberry, *Sorting the Smoke*

Terese Svoboda, *Laughing Africa*

1990

Philip Dacey, *Night Shift at the Crucifix Factory*

Lynda Hull, *Star Ledger*

1991

Greg Pape, *Sunflower Facing the Sun*

Walter Pavlich, *Running near the End of the World*

1992

Lola Haskins, *Hunger*

Katherine Soniat, *A Shared Life*

1993

Tom Andrews, *The Hemophiliac's Motorcycle*

Michael Heffernan, *Love's Answer*

John Wood, *In Primary Light*

1994

James McKean, *Tree of Heaven*

Bin Ramke, *Massacre of the Innocents*

Ed Roberson, *Voices Cast Out to Talk Us In*

1995

Ralph Burns, *Swamp Candles*

Maureen Seaton, *Furious Cooking*

1996

Pamela Alexander, *Inland*

Gary Gildner, *The Bunker in the Parsley Fields*

John Wood, *The Gates of the Elect Kingdom*

1997

Brendan Galvin, *Hotel Malabar*

Leslie Ullman, *Slow Work through Sand*

1998

Kathleen Peirce, *The Oval Hour*

Bin Ramke, *Wake*

Cole Swensen, *Try*